TEN ZEN QUESTIONS

TEN ZEN
QUESTIONS

Susan Blackmore

ONEWORLD

OXFORD

A Oneworld Book

Published by Oneworld Publications 2009

Copyright © Susan Blackmore 2009

Illustrations © Susan Blackmore 2009

ISBN 978–1–85168–642–1

Typeset by Jayvee, Trivandrum, India
Cover design by www.edwardbettison.com
Printed and bound in Great Britain by TJ International

Oneworld Publications
185 Banbury Road
Oxford OX2 7AR
England
www.oneworld-publications.com

Mixed Sources
Product group from well-managed
forests and other controlled sources
www.fsc.org Cert no. SGS-COC-2482
© 1996 Forest Stewardship Council

Contents

Acknowledgements

I want to thank many people who contributed, in ways they may not even know about, to the writing of this book. Several people read early drafts and provided helpful comments and suggestions. Others just inspired me with their understanding.

My thanks go to Reb Anderson, Stephen Batchelor, Guy Claxton, Peter Coonradt, John Crook, Peter and Elizabeth Fenwick, Mike Finch, Adam Hart-Davis, Mike Luetchford, Jack Petranker, Emily Troscianko, and to Mandy Little, my agent, and Marsha Filion, my editor at Oneworld.

Falling into Zen

Thinking in not thinking

Thinking is fun. Indeed, you could say that thinking is the joy of my life, and my favourite hobby. But thinking clearly is difficult, and most of us are not really taught how to do it.

Science needs clear thinking, and scientists have to construct logical arguments, think critically, ask awkward questions, and find the flaws in other people's arguments, but somehow they are expected to do all this without any kind of preliminary mental training. Certainly science courses do not begin with a session on calming the mind.

Perhaps this does not matter. If you are intelligent and quick witted it is possible to push away unwanted thoughts for a time, and to make great intellectual leaps or carry out painstaking experiments, even with a cluttered mind, but some questions demand a different approach. Among them are the ones I am asking here; questions that ask about the obvious – 'What is this? Where is this?'; those that turn back on themselves such as 'Who is asking the question?'; or those that ask about the nature of the asking mind itself. All these require a clarity of mind that is not necessary for most scientific questions. They seem to require both the capacity to think and the capacity to refrain from thinking.

Refraining from thinking is precisely the skill that is taught in meditation. In many traditions too much thinking is discouraged, and with good reason, because people frequently grasp ideas intellectually but fail to put them into practice. They may understand a difficult concept, but not shift their way of seeing the world. So, for example, Buddhist teachers often punish their students for thinking too much. On the other hand, using meditation to think is not entirely unknown in Buddhist practice, and it is clear that the Buddha himself was a deep thinker. In any case, my aim here was not to achieve enlightenment, or to transcend suffering, but to explore ten difficult questions; and for this purpose I needed to combine thinking with not thinking.

Alongside my science I have explored many alternative world views from witchcraft to spiritualism and Theosophy to chakras, but in spite of their superficial appeal they all proved deeply unsatisfactory. They provided answers all right, but the answers were dogmatic and confusing; they didn't fit with scientific understanding, and neither did they lead to any new discoveries. Worst of all, their doctrines did not change in response to change, but remained rigidly dependent on ancient books or the claims of their proponents. That is, until I stumbled across Zen. I was encouraged to have 'Great Doubt', told to 'Investigate!', and taught how to do it.

Zen is a branch of Buddhism that began as 'Chan' in seventh-century China and later spread east to become known as Zen in Japan. Although based on the teachings and insights of the historical Buddha, Zen puts far less emphasis on theory and studying texts than do other branches of Buddhism, and far more on practising meditation to gain direct experience of one's true nature.

This may be why, from its appearance in the West in the late nineteenth century, Zen has appealed to academics, philosophers and other thinkers who enjoy its strange paradoxes and who don't want to be involved in religious practices or dogmatic beliefs.

Like science, Zen demands that you ask questions, apply disciplined methods of inquiry, and overthrow any ideas that don't fit with what you find out. Indeed Zen is just like science in being more a set of techniques than a body of dogma. Zen has its doctrines and science its theories but in both cases these are temporary attempts to understand the universe, pending deeper inquiry and further discovery. Zen does not demand that you believe anything or have blind faith, but that you work hard to find out for yourself.

I am not a Buddhist. I have not joined any Buddhist orders, adopted any religious beliefs, nor taken any formal vows. I say this now because I do not want anyone to think I am writing under false pretences. Nothing I say here should be taken as the words of a Zen Buddhist. Rather, I am someone with a questioning mind who has stumbled upon Zen and found it immensely helpful. It has pushed me further and further into the kind of questions I have always asked – including the ones I have chosen to tackle here. They are the sort of questions which concern the very mind that is asking the question.

This book is an exploration of ten of my favourite questions and where they took me. It is also my attempt to see whether looking directly into one's own mind can contribute to a science of consciousness. Bringing personal experience into science is positively frowned upon in most of science; and with good reason. If you want to find out the truth about planetary motion, the human genome or the effectiveness of a new medicine, then personal beliefs are a hindrance not a help. However, this may not be true for all of science. As our growing understanding of the brain brings us ever closer to facing up to the problem of consciousness, it may be time for the scientist's own experience to be welcomed as part of the science itself, if only as a guide to theorising or to provide a better description of what needs to be explained. This book describes my own attempt to combine science and personal practice in the investigation of consciousness.

I shall explain the methods of inquiry I used and how I learned to practise them before turning to the questions themselves, but if you want to skip straight to the questions then please do.

Calming the mind

Asking these ten Zen questions both requires and encourages a calm mind. But minds tend not to be calm. Indeed they tend to rush about, full of overlapping thoughts, pushed here and there by emotional responses, irritated by tunes that go round and round, and generally flashing from one thing to another. It is not possible to tackle any question steadily and deeply with a mind in turmoil.

How, then, can the mind be calmed? Meditation is the obvious answer, and is the method I have used here. Learning to meditate means nothing more than learning to sit still and pay attention, staying relaxed and alert, without getting tangled up in trains of thought, emotions or inner conversations. I learned to meditate partly out of curiosity, and partly because I was driven by the pain and confusion of life, and thought that meditation might help.

Later I discovered that in Zen there are techniques for training the mind to look hard, and stick steadfastly to asking questions; difficult questions. The Zen method of inquiry at first seemed quite separate from my science, and even antithetical to it, but gradually I came to realise how compatible the two methods are.

As a student, in the 1970s, I learned the meditation practice called 'Zazen', described as 'just sitting'. I assumed that sitting still, alert and relaxed, and doing nothing would be easy, but instead I learned how hard it is. I wanted to keep trying but, like many people, I failed to get into a regular habit of meditation. Then in 1980 I went to evening classes held in the basement of his Bristol home by John Crook, a distinguished university lecturer and also a Zen teacher. John was a teacher I could be comfortable with; not a shaven-headed, mysterious master from the East but a down-to-earth, English academic who had trained with monks and Zen masters and was now adapting his understanding for Westerners like myself. Sometimes it is the oddest things that stick in the mind. I remember sitting there one evening with a group of other novice meditators, struggling to get comfortable, sitting cross-legged on my cushion and looking down at the bare wall in front of me in the standard Zen fashion, when he said that our minds should be so calm that we would hear a woodlouse crawling across the floor. Somehow this stuck with me and I wanted to be able to hear that woodlouse. I suppose the idea made me realise how much turmoil there was in my mind. There was no silence in which to hear such a tiny noise.

A couple of years later I went on my first retreat at John's farmhouse in mid Wales. Maenllwyd (pronounced man-thloyd) is a tiny, solid, stone house, nestling in a little cwm or valley, just below the edge of the moor. All around it the sheep graze among the grey rocks and heather, chomping and bleating. Reached by a few miles of rough track meandering between the fields, the house has no electricity, no gas, no phone, and not even mobile phone reception. It is cold there, even in summer, the outlook is bleak, and the nearest tiny village is miles away down the valley.

The house itself is full of ancient furniture, decorated with sheep skulls and bones, lit by oil lamps, and heated by an ancient kitchen range that belches out smoke when the wind is in the wrong direction. Meals are eaten in silence in what was once a small barn, and retreatants sleep on wooden platforms above. Across the rough, unpaved farmyard with its mud and sheep pens, is another barn now converted into a meditation hall.

When I went on my first retreat in 1982, the pipes all froze, the roof was in urgent need of repair, and the wind blew right through the barn where we slept. Owls flew in, and the bats roosted just above us. That January the snow was fifteen feet deep down in the valley and a snowplough had cut through just as far as the nearest farm below. It was there that we left our cars and trudged up through the fields. I was given a walking stick to help me, for I was eight months pregnant with my first child, Emily.

We meditated for many hours each day, in half-hour sessions with brief breaks in between, huddled in blankets in the subzero house with our breaths visibly steaming in the cold air. We longed for the work periods when you could get warm splitting wood, or beating carpets, or even chopping vegetables in the kitchen near the range. I got the chance I had wanted – to get away and contemplate myself and my life before motherhood. But I also got far more than I had bargained for. Perhaps I expected that, with a whole week of practice, meditation would become easy and I'd be quickly transformed into a superior person or even become enlightened. Instead, the long hours of sitting exposed the horrible mess in my mind; the visions, the fears, the anger and resentment, the guilt, the worries and the perplexity.

Now I understood the need for a calm mind. We were told that calming the mind is the starting point of all meditation, but that it can also take you all the way. We were told even scarier things; that what you are searching for is here right now, that there is really nothing to strive for, and that once you arrive you will realise there was nowhere to go in the first place; that however hard you work, and you must work hard, in the end you will know that there is nothing to be done.

To explain the Zen method more clearly, John used to say 'Let it come. Let it be. Let it go.' This roughly means – when any ideas or feelings or troubles come along in meditation, don't fight them, don't engage with them, don't push them away or hang onto them, just go through this same gentle process again and again: let them arise in the mind, let them be whatever they are without elaboration, and let them go in their own time. Then they cause you no trouble and the mind stays still – however beautiful or horrible they are.

Paying attention and letting go sounds so simple and so easy. It is neither, as I quickly discovered. Hour after hour we retreatants sat there on our cushions trying to calm the mind; letting go and paying attention. Again and again my mind would slip

to thoughts about the past or the future; to imaginary conversations with other people; to rerunning something I had done to
make it seem better; to planning how to make amends for actions
that I felt bad about. 'Let it go …'. Again and again, I would slip
into half-sleep and the cracks in the plaster on the ancient wall in
front of me would turn into gruesome visions of horror and war
and torture and suffering; over and over, again and again. 'Let it be
…'. One day John said 'Remember there is only you and the wall,
and the wall isn't doing it.'

Mindfulness

Mindfulness is usually described as 'being in the present moment'.
When I first heard of this idea, at a conference on Buddhism and
psychology, I thought it very strange because surely I was already
in the present moment wasn't I? Where else could I be? But then
I started asking myself 'Am I in the present moment now?' and
noticed something very odd: the answer was always 'yes' but I got
the peculiar feeling that perhaps a moment ago I had not been
present at all. It was a bit like waking up. But if so, from what?

I wondered whether trying to stay present for longer would
bring about some kind of continuity from moment to moment.
For the sense of continuity, which I had taken for granted without
even thinking about it, seemed threatened by this suspicion that
I was frequently not there at all. And where was I if not here?
Was ordinary life a kind of dream you could wake up from? All

sorts of questions poured up and I had no idea what to do with them.

I was also acutely aware of my own troubled mind. At that time we were living in Germany where my husband was working while I stayed at home with our two small children, and tried to learn German. I longed to find time on my own to write. I felt isolated, unhappy and, above all, unreal. Nothing seemed alive or vibrant. Our flat in the picturesque town of Tübingen looked out over a beautiful park and I used to stare at the trees, pinching myself to try to make them seem real, feeling guilty for not appreciating them. I loathed this unreality. I felt I was not truly there at all. Certainly I was not 'in the present moment'.

So when I heard about mindfulness, I decided, right there at the conference, to try it. 'OK' I thought to myself 'how long shall I try it for ... an hour? a day?' But that would be to miss the point. If I were to be truly in the present moment I could only do it now, and then now, and then now. So I began.

The effect was startling – and then frightening. Being in the present moment, which had seemed so uncontroversial in prospect, was terrifying in practice. It meant giving up so much – in fact practically everything. It meant that I was not to think about the next moment, not to dwell on what I had just done, not to think about what I might have said instead, not to imagine a conversation that I might have later, not to look forward to lunch, not to look forward to weekends, or holidays or ... anything. But the idea had grabbed me and I kept doing it. In fact I kept doing it for seven weeks.

Most of this process seemed to be about giving up or letting go. As my mind slipped from the world in front of me to thoughts about the past or the future, a little voice inside would say 'Come back to the present', or 'Be here now', or 'Let it go'. I remembered John's saying 'Let it come. Let it be. Let it go.' Now I was doing this for real, not just in sitting meditation or on retreat, but in every moment of every day. Everything had to be let go of, apart from whatever was right there, arising in the present moment. I found myself saying 'Let it ...' or just 'Le ...' and staying fully present, right here.

There is something truly awful about having to let go of so much. Sometimes in bed at night I just wanted to give in – to indulge in some easy sexual fantasy, or pleasant speculation – but the little voice kept going, 'Le...'. Then odd things began to happen. First of all, I had assumed (without much thinking about it) that all those endless thoughts about what I had just done and what I had to do next were necessary for living my complicated life. Now I found they were not. I was amazed at just how much mental energy I had been using up when so little is required. To take a simple example, I found that I could go through a series of thoughts such as 'I think I'll make a butter bean casserole for supper. I've got tomatoes and carrots indoors but I must remember to go out and pick some broccoli before dark' in a flash, and then drop it, and still remember to go and get the broccoli later on. Why had I been wasting so much effort before?

Another oddity was to realise that the present moment is always all right. This bizarre, but liberating, notion crept up on me gradually. Time and again I noticed that all my troubles lay in the thoughts I was letting go of – not in the immediate situation. Even if the immediate situation was a difficult one, the difficulties almost always concerned the past or the future. For example, I was annoyed that, yet again, the heating oil had run out and I was the one who had to take the can three flights down to the cellar to fetch more, but the steps in front of me and the sight of my feet climbing the stairs were fine. I might be bored and anxious trying to fit in with the other kindergarten Mums but the sounds of children playing, and the kindergarten door in front of me were fine. I might be rushing in a panic for a bus, worrying what would happen and how to apologise if I missed it, but the running feet and scenes flashing by were fine.

Of course, difficult situations have to be dealt with, but oddly enough even these seemed easier, rather than harder, when I was paying attention to the now. I found myself, when faced with one particularly difficult life decision, writing down a list of pros and cons and assessing them. But this was done in a completely new way: I thought through the likely consequences of each decision in turn, paying fierce attention to each one on the list. Then I decided on one of them, without agonising or trying to go back on the decision. Then I got on with the one that had been chosen.

Letting go of what you've done immediately afterwards is enormously freeing but, in conventional terms, rather worrying. A natural fear is that you will behave idiotically, make a fool of yourself, do something dangerous or, more worrying still, that you will let go of all moral responsibility. Oddly enough this did not seem to happen. Indeed, the body seemed to keep on doing relevant and sensible things, apparently without all the agonising I had assumed was essential. Time and again I found that my mind had summed up the options, chosen one, carried it out, and moved on. I didn't need to fret over every decision, or ask whether it was the 'right' thing to have done. It was past.

Being able to act and then move on may seem to mean letting go of all responsibility, yet responsible actions still happen. This interesting paradox re-emerges in some of the questions. Other paradoxes concern the sense of self. Right now, in this moment, things are happening, but when there are no thoughts about the past and future, there is little sense of someone who is experiencing them or doing them. Although I would have been frightened at such a prospect if anyone had told me about it, in practice it was like a previously unnoticed burden being lifted, or like the relief of a horrible sound stopping when you hadn't even noticed it was bothering you.

There were dangers. I remember once trying to cross a mountain road, holding my two-year-old's hand, and realising that I simply could not judge the speed of the oncoming cars. In the present moment they were frozen, and the next moment was not in my mind. I decided I must have gone a bit too far. I have no idea what happens if you push this even further, or let go of even more of the mind. I have no idea whether continuing this kind of practice all of one's life is either feasible or desirable, although there are many who advocate it. I only know that I worked hard at it for seven weeks and then stopped. Indeed the whole process seemed naturally to come to an end.

Finally, one simple fact I noticed was that instead of being a chore, sitting down to meditate was a blessed relief. It was much easier to just sit and pay attention to the present moment than it was to rush about, look after the children, drive the car, or write letters, while paying attention to the present moment. So from then on, although I gave up the intense mindfulness practice, I meditated every day. And finally, at last, things began to seem real again. The trees were right here and vivid and alive. The kids' shouts were immediate and full of energy, and I was right there with them and what they were doing. I seemed to be less of the self I thought I was before, but I (or someone) felt far more alive.

Continuing practice

I have never again worked with such intensity as I did all those years ago, but I have practised mindfulness on and off, and continue to meditate every day. Like mindfulness, meditation skills can easily be lost, or buried. So it is important to keep practising if you want to ask questions with a clear and calm mind. Just about everyone who meditates regularly says they have, or once had, trouble establishing regular daily practice. For me it was the encounter with mindfulness that made it possible, but some hints and tips from others also helped a lot. So I pass them on in case they are of any use.

Most important is not expecting too much of yourself. The Transcendental Meditation organisation, for example, recommends two periods of twenty minutes a day. Tibetan Buddhists are also expected to practise twice a day and to carry out visualisations intended to invoke mindfulness, compassion or insight at the start of hour-long sessions. Zen sessions are usually half an hour, but serious practitioners do several sessions a day with short breaks in between. This is easy on retreat, or at inspiring conferences, and if you go to one you may be tempted to think you can keep it up, but it is a big chunk of time out of a busy day, and if you fail you end up feeling bad about yourself and giving up altogether.

Personally I'm not prepared to give that much time outside of retreats, nor do I want to agonise each day about whether I'm going to sit or not. So I meditate for about 15 minutes a day, first thing in the morning, often with my partner, and this suits me well. It seems, gradually, to establish deep changes that I welcome, and it is – after all – a lot better than nothing. Most obviously, calming the mind becomes gradually easier. You may be able to do a lot more than I do and that would probably make for much deeper practice, but I am sure that a little is better than none, and every day is better than intermittently.

I was once helped greatly by someone who told me this 'Commit yourself to sitting on your cushion every day. That's all; if you want to stop after 3 seconds that's fine.' I found this rather odd advice extremely useful and that is the extent of my personal commitment now. There are, in fact, rare occasions when I sit for only a few seconds – for example, if I have overslept and have a train to catch, or when some crisis has just occurred. More often, if I don't feel like sitting, I still force myself onto the cushion, expecting to last only a few minutes, and then somehow, once I'm there, it seems quite pleasant. Five minutes goes by – or even fifteen. Either way I have stuck to my commitment, and have a regular practice that gradually deepens.

I have described some of my own practice here because it may be relevant to understanding the way I asked the questions. It should be clear that I have learned a variety of skills over the years, and that some, though not all, of them are part of traditional Zen training. This book is about how I have used these techniques to

tackle ten difficult questions; you might say, using consciousness
to look into itself.

The questions

The questions arose in various ways and I tackled them at different times and in different places. Some of them had largely intellectual roots and emerged from my scientific studies. For example
the first question 'Am I conscious now?' is an obvious starting
point when you are battling intellectually with the mystery of consciousness. Yet even this simple question starts to have odd
effects if you keep asking it.

The second, 'What was in my consciousness a moment ago?'
was inspired by the effect of that first question on the students
who took my consciousness course. To get them looking into
their own experience as well as studying theory, I gave them a
series of questions as weekly exercises. They had to ask themselves the questions many times a day, all week, and I did the same.
Their explorations and difficulties inspired me greatly, and I
worked on these questions again and again in the years to come.

By contrast some of the questions are classic Buddhist ones.
One comes from the Mahamudra tradition of Tibetan Buddhism;
that is 'What is the difference between the mind resting in tranquillity and the mind moving in thought?', along with the related
question 'How does thought arise?' Over the years I have done
three formal Mahamudra retreats with John at Maenllwyd, and
this question is one of a series he uses. I found these questions

haunting me and so one year I decided to tackle the Mahamudra series again on my own.

I did this on solitary retreat at Maenllwyd. I had long been finding the formal retreats irksome, with so many people around, and so little sleep allowed. I wanted to meditate all alone in the mountains, in my own time, even if the prospect was a bit scary. By this time I knew John well. We had run university courses together, formed a group of academics interested in Buddhism, and I had been to Maenllwyd many times. So, on several occasions, John let me use the house on my own. I took enough food and other provisions, and spent five or six days there completely alone. I always went in summer so that I didn't have to struggle with oil lamps, or risk burning the place down with untended candles. I have had a temperamental kitchen range myself and so was able to cope with the vagaries of the ancient Rayburn. I kept milk and yogurt in the stream, other provisions in the mouse-proof boxes, and managed quite well.

Before I went I drew up a daily routine, mostly of half-hour sitting periods with short breaks between, but I also took a walk in the afternoon so that I could go up into the hills, and breaks for meals and doing jobs for John, such as cutting the long grass or chopping wood. I took no reading materials apart from the few pages of Mahamudra text, and tried to be mindful as much as I could. I should say that this is a somewhat daunting experience, out in the mountains completely alone, but it makes for very intense practice.

The final two questions are classic Zen koans. There is a long tradition in Zen of koan stories, often tales of strange interactions between masters and monks, with perplexing endings or intellectually nonsensical twists. In a classic example the master Hui Neng asks a monk, 'Without thinking of good or evil, show me your original face before your mother and father were born.'

In one of my favourites, an exhausted monk arrives at a monastery gate, after long travels through the mountains, to be met with a pointing finger and the question 'What is this thing and how did it get here?'

Koans are used to help shake the student out of attachment or complacency, to inspire insight, or to motivate the 'great doubt'. John's own teacher, Sheng Yen stresses 'Great faith, great doubt and great angry determination' as the basis of Zen practice. Koans can inspire all of these, as I learned on a series of koan retreats, where you work on the same question for a whole week. I found the koans very powerful, which may be why they have survived through many centuries and can still be helpful to people like you and me, in vastly different cultures from that in which they were first conceived.

Some of the other questions have obsessed me for a long time; whether they came out of my scientific work or arose in meditation. One day I decided to have a systematic go at them, and push them as far as I could in a limited time. So I gave myself a week's solitary retreat at home.

We have a fairly big garden, with vegetables, a small orchard, a greenhouse and a wooden 'summerhouse'; really more like a fancy garden shed. It's lined with old and faded velvet curtains; and with the addition of a mat, cushion, meditation stool and a few other things, was easily turned into a meditation hut. It was mid-winter at the time and I didn't want to freeze, so I also took a kettle, tea things, a hot water bottle and a few other comforts. Although I slept indoors, I determinedly avoided the phone, email, post and any other distractions when I went indoors at night, and otherwise I just stayed out there in the garden all day.

I set myself a simple routine of half-hour sitting periods interspersed with short breaks, or periods of working mindfully in the garden. I spent the first day just calming the mind, and then set myself one question each day. In a day, consisting of about six hours of meditation, I could make considerable progress with one of these questions and record what happened. I had, of course, already been working on the questions in various ways for many years, but it was helpful to concentrate my efforts this way. When I was writing the book I went back out to the shed several times for a day or more to have another go at the questions.

Although the questions and the situations differed widely, I have found myself settling into a method of inquiry that (although it may not suit others) seems to let my science and my Zen practice illuminate each other.

In most cases the method I used is something like this. Having chosen the question to work on, I forget all about it, and just sit and let the mind calm down a little. Once thoughts have slowed (after perhaps fifteen or twenty minutes) I begin to apply a little pressure; concentrating harder on the present moment, for example. I then sit for a while, letting this stabilise into an alert and open state. I am awake, able to concentrate, but with few distractions. It is certainly possible to have an absolutely clear mind, with no thoughts at all, but I am still not very good at this and, happily, it is not entirely necessary for this sort of thinking. As long as the mind is open, spacious, calm and steady – and any distractions are easily dropped – then I'm ready for the question.

Just how this comes about I don't know, but at some point the question just pops up. It has been stored away there, waiting to be asked, and now jumps in. So I begin tackling it, and I do so in a thoroughly systematic way. Some questions lead to a vast branching tree of demanding possibilities. For example, 'There is no time; what is memory?' is just seven words and yet opens up a whole world of possible lines to explore. You can agree with the statement and ask the question; disagree with the statement and ask the question; explore time; explore memory; or use the whole as an opening to timelessness. I usually mentally set out the obvious tasks first, commit the plan to memory, and then start on the branches one by one. Each then leads to more, and it requires considerable practice (though very little time) to keep a plan of the route in mind while exploring the branches. But this is the fun of thinking, and I love it.

Other questions require less planning and more direct experience. For example, 'What is the difference between the mind resting in tranquillity and the mind moving in thought?' is a real killer (presumably this is why it is used in Mahamudra training). It sounds, at first reading, like a question that might have an answer, but then you realise that to answer it you must be familiar with the mind resting in tranquillity – not easy. Then you must be able to observe the mind moving in thought – tricky in a totally different way. Then you, presumably, have to compare them. By this time the question itself seems unimportant and the exploration of the groundwork far more so.

I said that asking the questions both requires and encourages a calm mind, and these examples explain why. A calm mind is necessary for the sort of determined, systematic thinking that I am talking about; otherwise you just get distracted and lose track. But then the questions themselves often provoke further calming – not because thinking is calming; it isn't; but because of the subject matter. A question such as 'Where is this experience?' requires a steady experience to look into. Those such as 'Who is asking the question?' or 'Am I conscious now?' can defeat all logical thought and hurl the mind into emptiness.

I am explaining this partly to show how I set about the ten questions, but partly to make it clear that my approach is not that advocated in most Zen training. Indeed in Zen one is often reminded that 'thought is the enemy' and in general all kinds of thinking are discouraged. I did a lot of thinking because it was the best tool I had available for exploring the ten questions, and because this kind of thinking forms a bridge between my Zen practice and my science. I have dared to call them 'Zen questions' because I believe they all get right to the point of the Zen endeavour; to expose the nature of self and mind, and to realise nonduality.

Maenllwyd

The problem of consciousness

*C*onsciousness is said to be the greatest mystery facing science today. The mystery is as old as philosophy itself and has never been satisfactorily solved – it is, in one form or another, the mind–body problem; the familiar problem of dualism.

The trouble is this: take any object you like; you might pick up a pen or a book, or a glass of wine if you happen to have one to hand as you read (I do as I write). Now look at it hard. It seems impossible not to believe that this is a real physical object inhabiting a real physical world, in time and space, and with properties and laws that apply to everyone. After all, the glass of wine behaves in predictable ways; if you let go it will drop onto the floor with a crash and make a mess; if you hand it to someone else they will say 'Thank you' and agree that it's a glass of 2005 claret and tastes full and fruity with a touch of tannin. It's hard to explain any of this without assuming a physical world containing actual wine.

But now turn to your own experience. Raise your glass to the light and enjoy the deep, glinting red as it appears through the glass; lift it to your nose and smell the unique mixture of aromas. Taste it. These qualities are what you, and you alone, experience in the privacy of your own mind. You have no idea how the wine tastes or smells to your friend, whether that particular red looks to her the way it does to you, or even whether her experience of red is more like your experience of blue (to raise an old philosophical conundrum). It's hard to think about any of this without assuming a private mental world.

Philosophers refer to these private mental qualities (the redness of the red wine, the scent or the feel of the glass on your skin) as qualia. Some philosophers reject the existence of qualia but even they agree that what we mean by 'consciousness' is subjective experience. A famous paper in the 1970s asked, 'What is it like to be a bat?' The answer is that we cannot really know what it's like, but we can agree that if there is anything it is like to be a bat, then the bat is conscious. If there is nothing it is like to be the bat (or a stone or a baby or a glass of wine) then the bat is not conscious. To be conscious means to have subjective experiences: to say that I am conscious means that there is something it is like to be me.

So we really are stuck with two completely different kinds of thing – physical things in the world and subjective experiences. They just don't match up. They seem to be so different.

You might like to accept that they are different, and that the world just does consist of two fundamentally different kinds of stuff. If so you will not be alone. Indeed belief in dualism seems to be the natural state of human thinking about the world. Ideas about spirits and souls, and transcendent mental realms, are found in historical documents going back thousands of years, and dualism prevails in most societies that survive on the planet today.

Even in the wealthy and educated West, surveys of the general population show that most people are dualists: that is, they believe that mind and body are separate, or that they have an inner self that is something above and beyond the mere physical shell. It's so tempting.

Many people also believe that their mind can influence their body. Although this sounds reasonable, in fact it implies that the two are separate things. So it's a hidden form of dualism. Then many believe that their spirit, or soul, can survive the death of the physical body. This kind of dualism is often sold as the 'spiritual' way of seeing the world, as opposed to the 'anti-spiritual' scientific view. It is promoted in countless new age and 'mind and spirit' books and magazines, and set against the supposedly heartless materialism of science. Yet claiming to be spiritual does not make it so, and these lucrative world views rarely even acknowledge the difficulties, let alone try to solve them, as both science and Zen try to do.

The most famous failed solution is the 'Cartesian dualism' proposed by the seventeenth-century French philosopher, René Descartes. He thought that the physical body was a clever machine made of physical stuff. In this he was well ahead of his time, but he could not account for free will and consciousness, and so he concluded that the mind was something completely different and was made of mental, thinking, non-physical stuff. The enduring problem for Cartesian dualism, which has never been solved, is that if these two stuffs really are so different then they cannot interact with each other. And if they cannot interact then the theory cannot explain what needs to be explained – that my mind perceives what my physical eyes and ears detect, and my thoughts seem to give rise to my body's actions. Descartes thought that the two interacted in the pineal gland, but he could not say how. Nor could anyone else. So dualism doesn't help. It's a cop out.

You may want to squirm out of this painful problem – and do try. There are two obvious directions to take and both have been thoroughly explored. On the one hand you might try idealism; the idea that there is no separate physical world, and everything in the universe is made up of thoughts, or ideas or consciousness. But then what gives the physical world its stable properties, and why do we all agree that the wine glass fell to the floor and broke, or that it weighed 27 grams and is made of lead crystal? On the other hand you might try materialism; the idea that there is no separate mental world, and everything in the universe is made of matter. The majority of scientists (though not all) claim to be materialists, but then what can our subjective experiences be? How can the exquisite taste of this wine be a physical thing?

This brings us to a modern version of the mind–body problem, called the 'Hard Problem' of consciousness: that is, how can objective, physical processes in the brain give rise to subjective experience? Neuroscientists are making tremendous progress in understanding the objective brain processes; with brain scans, implanted electrodes, computer models, and all sorts of other ways of investigating how the brain works. We can measure the electrical firing of neurons, the chemical behaviour in synapses, the processing of information, and the mechanisms of vision, hearing, and memory. We can see how information flows in through the senses, and how responses are coordinated and actions carried out.

But what about me and my conscious experiences? Where do I fit into this integrated system of inputs, outputs and multiple parallel processing systems? The strange thing is that I feel as if I am in the middle of all this activity, experiencing what comes in through the senses, and deciding what to do in response, when in fact the brain seems to have no need of me. There is no central place or process where I could be, and the brain seems capable of doing everything it does without any supervisor, decider or inner experiencer. Indeed, the more we learn about how the brain works the more it seems that something is left out – that very thing we care about most of all – 'consciousness itself'.

Is there really such a thing? This question divides the field of consciousness studies more acutely than any other. Almost every scientist and philosopher today rejects dualism in principle, yet many still believe that we need special explanations for consciousness and that understanding learning, memory or perception is not enough. Others are convinced that when we understand all the physical processes there will be nothing left over – consciousness will have been explained – and accuse the first group of being closet dualists. And so the impasse remains.

Nonduality

The temptation to fall into dualism is so strong that escaping from it, and from the popular idea that we have a spirit or soul, has been a rare insight in human history. This insight is not confined to modern science and philosophy, but can be found at the heart of Christian mysticism, Sufism, Advaita, Taoism and Buddhism. All these traditions claim that the apparent duality of the world is an illusion, and that underlying the illusion everything is one.

Along with this often goes the idea that there is no separate self who acts, so that realising nonduality also means giving up the sense of personal action or of being the 'doer' of what happens. This is rather hard to accept, which is probably why such traditions are so much less popular than the great theistic religions, or those that promise heaven and hell to reward the actions of individual souls.

Right at the heart of Buddhist teaching is the idea that all apparent forms are really empty of inherent selfhood or independent existence; and yet emptiness itself is none other than form. This applies to everything we experience, including all sensations, perceptions, actions and consciousness, and is especially important when applied to the self. A popular metaphor describes the self as like the collection of parts that make up a carriage. We give the collection a name, we call it a carriage, but we accept that there is nothing more to it than the wheels, chassis, body and all the other parts. In a similar way, the human body is just such a collection of parts; heart, lungs, liver, muscles, brain and sinews; there is no additional separate self inside. Yet we find this much harder to accept.

Along with this goes the idea that, although these collections of parts carry out actions, there is no inner 'doer' or actor in addition to the actions themselves. This is wonderfully clear in the Buddhist saying 'Actions exist, and also their consequences, but the person that acts does not.'

All branches of Buddhism refer to this central idea, although it seems to get rather lost in popular versions of Tibetan Buddhism, which describe reincarnation as though there were a separate person living many lives. The Buddha seems to reject this appealing idea in saying 'There is no one to cast away this set of elements, and no one to assume a new set of them.' Chan and Zen, in particular, face up to this. Dogen, the thirteenth-century Zen master and founder of Soto Zen, said 'To study the way of the Buddha is to study your own self. To study your own self is to forget yourself. To forget yourself is to have the objective world prevail in you.' This, then, is to arrive at nondual awareness, or to realise nonduality.

In the end this is the aim of Chan and Zen practice. Perhaps this is why I knew I had stumbled upon something special when I first encountered Zen. Like the science I had been learning, and like the results of my own inner struggles, it rejected the common view of a mind that inhabits a body. In its place it put only a world – and questions and more questions.

Modern science and Buddhism may share the aim of under-standing the world without recourse to dualism, but the methods they use are entirely different and so are their objectives. While sci-ence advocates thinking, hypothesising, and testing by experiment, Buddhism rejects thinking and delights in paradox. While science aims at understanding, prediction and control, Buddhist practice aims at directly realising nonduality and thus escaping from delusion and suffering into enlightenment. I have no idea whether these aims are ultimately compatible or not but I have set out to work on these questions on the assumption that they might be, and that meditation practice might actually help illuminate the science.

The science of consciousness

As we have seen, most scientists and philosophers agree that the problem of consciousness is all about 'What it's like to be', and so they try to understand how an objective, physical brain can give rise to subjective awareness. They try to avoid dualism, and yet this proves to be very hard.

For all the many differences in theories of consciousness, there are some underlying assumptions that almost all scientists make. For example, they assume that at any time in someone's waking experience, some of their brain processes are conscious but many more are not. The former are said to be 'in consciousness', 'in awareness', or are part of the 'contents of consciousness': the latter are 'outside consciousness', 'below the level of awareness', or are 'subconscious' or 'unconscious'. If this is the right way to think about the mind, then science needs to explain the difference, and indeed many scientists are trying. In particular they are looking for the 'neural correlates of consciousness', the functions of consciousness and the reasons why consciousness evolved.

Although none of these assumptions may sound problematic, I believe they are. Let's take the idea of the 'contents of consciousness'. This popular phrase simply indicates the apparently obvious fact that at any time there are some things I am conscious of and some I am not; and maybe there are others in a kind of twilight zone. We give names to these such as conscious, unconscious, subconscious, semi-conscious, preconscious and so on. This implies that consciousness is like a space or container – that there are processes going on inside the brain that are unconscious until they get 'into' consciousness.

This fits well with some common metaphors. One is the idea of the 'stream of consciousness'. This comes from the nineteenth-century psychologist, William James, who said that consciousness does not feel to itself to be chopped up in bits, but seems to flow, like a river or stream. He went on to reject many common assumptions about consciousness, but his notion of the stream stuck.

Another common metaphor is the 'theatre of consciousness'. I may feel as though I am watching events on my own personal stage, lighting some up with the spotlight of my attention, while others lurk in the shadows, jump onto the stage to demand attention, or come into my consciousness and then slip off the stage again into the darkness.

Many theories have been built on theatre models, the best known of which is 'Global workspace' theory. First described by psychologist Bernard Baars, and subsequently elaborated and tested by many other researchers, the basic idea is that the brain is organised around a workspace in which important information is processed on something like the stage in a theatre. Items that are processed in this workspace are then broadcast to the rest of the (unconscious) brain, and this global availability is what makes them conscious.

'What's wrong with that?', you might ask. I think the answer depends on how literally you take the theatre metaphor. The philosopher, Dan Dennett, points out the dangers of imagining what he calls the 'Cartesian theatre'. He suggests that although almost all scientists and philosophers reject Cartesian dualism, many still hang onto the metaphors that it implies, including the theatre. We imagine ourselves, says Dennett, as an audience of one, in our private mental theatre, where our experiences come into our consciousness and then leave it again, in a continuous stream of thoughts, ideas, perceptions, memories and desires. But what could these correspond to in a real brain? There is no central place in the brain where 'I' could be; it's just millions of neurons all interconnected in billions of ways. There is no screen where the visions could appear; no single place where 'consciousness happens', and no central command headquarters where 'I' could make all my decisions, because decisions are made all over the brain. So if you imagine a theatre, a stream of experiences and an observer, then you are doomed to fail to find them.

Dennett describes the self as a 'benign user illusion', and replaces the theatre with his theory of 'multiple drafts'. According to this theory, the brain processes events in multiple ways, all in parallel and in different versions. None of the drafts is 'in consciousness' or 'outside consciousness'; they appear so only when the system is probed in some way, such as by provoking a response or asking a question. Only then is one of the many drafts taken as what the person must have been conscious of. This is why he claims that 'There are no fixed facts about the stream of consciousness independent of particular probes.'

Multiple drafts theory really is difficult to understand, perhaps because its implications are so profound. It means that if you ask 'What was I conscious of a moment ago?' there is no right answer: it depends on what happens next. Indeed, there may be no answer to the question 'What was I conscious of then?' during most of your life. Only when you have to give a response or answer a question do you, or someone else, conclude that you were conscious of a particular thing or event. That thing or event is then taken to be the contents of your consciousness, but it would not have been had you not been asked. It was never 'in' or 'out' of something called consciousness.

Dennett calls those who still believe in the Cartesian theatre 'Cartesian materialists'; they claim to be materialists and not to believe in separate selves or any spooky mental stuff, but by falling for the theatre imagery they are imagining an impossibility.

Not surprisingly no one admits to being a Cartesian materialist. Baars, for example, protests that the global workspace is a real working part of the brain, not a Cartesian theatre. But if it is part of the brain (or a particular process in the brain) then the hard problem remains; how does this part, or process, give rise to subjective experiences? Why does being globally broadcast mean information becomes conscious?

This is just one example, but hints of Cartesian materialism can be found in just about every discussion of consciousness. Such phrases as 'in consciousness', 'represented in awareness', and 'the contents of consciousness', all imply Cartesian materialism.

Dennett's ideas are very well known, and also much hated. He has been called the devil of consciousness studies, and his book *Consciousness Explained* derided as 'Consciousness Explained Away'. People seem to think that his brand of materialism is deeply unspiritual, or even anti-spiritual, and is the least likely to be compatible with meditation practice or mystical insights.

I disagree, for what Dennett is really trying to do is to point out some of the traps that we so easily fall into when thinking about consciousness, just as Zen points out the delusions we so easily fall into. I think Dennett is right about these traps, but I would add that the reason we so easily fall into them is that we assume we know what consciousness is like. We may think, 'I am conscious now, so I must know what my own consciousness is like, and no one can tell me otherwise.' But perhaps we don't. And if we don't then all of this grand scientific enterprise may be trying to explain the wrong things. This is why I suggest we might look again into our own minds, and indeed why I have spent so much of my time doing just that.

Seeing the world

Vision seems so simple. We open our eyes and there is the world. Yet scientists have long appreciated how difficult this is to explain. For a start, we move our eyes about five or six times a second, fixating on something and then moving quickly on, but we don't notice this, and the world appears stable. Also we can see clearly only a tiny area around that fixation point, yet it feels as though we are seeing the whole visual scene at once. How does this work?

Information goes in through the eyes, along the optic nerve, through way stations in the mid-brain, and on up to the visual cortex. And then what happens? It's so tempting to think that a picture appears 'in consciousness' so that 'I' can see it, but that wouldn't explain anything. 'I' would have to be another little person who looked at the picture and then there would need to be another little person inside me to look at that picture, and so on into an infinite regress.

The idea of an inner observer has long been rejected, but the idea of an inner picture is more persistent. Yet this too is problematic. Suppose that right now, while you are reading this book, all the words changed into different words. Would you notice? Yes, of course you would. Suppose now that the words changed just as you moved your eyes. Would you notice then? Or suppose that they changed just as you blinked. Would you notice? Most people say they would, and are horrified to discover that they probably would not.

This is known as 'change blindness', and it is amazing how large the changes can be and still go unnoticed if they happen during an eye movement or blink. I have done experiments in which people failed to see a teddy bear appearing and disappearing on a chair because the picture moved at the same time as it changed. Other researchers have used grey flashes between changes or tested people using film clips. Psychologist Richard Wiseman has made a film in which most of the objects, and people's clothing, change colour during switches of camera angle without people noticing. It is even possible for one actor to replace another between cuts and the viewer not see anything amiss.

This is bizarre. We think we have a rich and detailed impression of the world as we look at it, and that we know what is there in front of our eyes. And yet we don't notice massive changes. Why not?

I think what's going on is that our false assumptions are being challenged. For example, it's easy to assume that looking around and seeing the world means having a rich and detailed visual impression inside our brains. But if that is true then we ought to notice when something obvious changes.

Could it be that we don't really create a rich and detailed picture of the world at all? Indeed, if we did it would amount to a kind of Cartesian materialism, and vision would be the show in the non-existent Cartesian theatre. But what else could vision be? There are many new theories trying to cope with these findings. Some suggest that there are no inner representations at all, some suggest fleeting and temporary representations, some claim that visual experiences survive as long as we pay attention to them but then fall back into nothingness. Most agree that the apparent continuity of the visual world is not really in our heads at all but is out there in the world itself. Inside our heads there are only scraps and temporary constructions, arising and falling away – we get the illusion of continuity and detail because we can always look again to check any detail we like, so we never notice how scrappy experience really is.

This question of whether we really do build pictures in the head is important for a major branch of consciousness research, the hunt for the 'neural correlates of consciousness'. The idea is to take a conscious experience and try to discover which brain process correlates with that experience. Scientists such as Nobel laureate Francis Crick and his colleague Christof Koch have been looking for the neural correlates of the 'vivid picture of the world we see in front of our eyes'. Neuroscientist Antonio Damasio wants to understand how 'the movie-in-the-brain is generated'. Popular as their approach is, it will not succeed if there is no such thing as 'the vivid picture we see in front of our eyes'.

A particularly challenging response to change blindness is the 'sensorimotor theory' of Kevin O'Regan and Alva Noë: one of several 'enactive theories' of vision. For them, vision is emphatically not to do with building up pictures in the head. Instead, seeing means mastering the contingencies between what you do and the information that comes in. So seeing is a skill, and you can only see something as long as you keep using that skill and actively interacting with the world. There is no persisting picture in the head, and no one to look at it, so any dualism between self and world disappears.

'But it doesn't feel like this!', you might protest, 'I don't just see scraps that disappear several times a second. I don't experience things only so long as I'm interacting with them. They stay there. I'm experiencing a rich visual impression of the world around me right now.'

But are you really? What is it really like to be you now, looking out at the world? Could it be, as these ideas suggest, that the richness and stability of your visual world is an illusion? Could your own private experience actually be so different from what you have always assumed? Could you doubt what seems so obviously true?

This is why I wanted to look so hard into the nature of my own experience. If vision cannot be the way I think it feels then I want to be quite sure just how it does feel.

What does consciousness do?

Imagine that someone throws you a ball and you reach up and catch it neatly. The natural and tempting way to think about this simple action is to imagine that first you consciously notice the ball coming towards you, and judge its speed and position, and then you consciously control the movements of your arms and hands to catch it. It's as though you're sitting somewhere inside your head, experiencing events and then deciding how to respond.

This is, again, a form of Cartesian materialism, involving a little me inside who is having a stream of conscious experiences and acting upon them. Quite apart from philosophical doubts, the science tells us it cannot be like this. The visual system consists of as many as forty parallel pathways taking different routes through the brain. Among these are two main paths, the dorsal stream that controls fast actions, and the slower ventral stream that perceives and recognises objects. So if you are playing tennis, riding a bike or catching that ball, your dorsal stream will ensure that you catch the ball long before you can have seen that a ball was coming.

Similar disconcerting conclusions come from the series of famous experiments carried out by neuroscientist, Ben Libet. He asked people to carry out the simple action of flexing their wrist at a time of their own choosing, and was then able to show that the motor areas of their brain began preparing to make the action nearly half a second before the time at which they judged they made the conscious decision to act. This general effect has been confirmed many times since, and with several different methods.

People have interpreted this finding in countless different ways. The most obvious conclusion is that free will must be illusory or that consciousness has no effect, but there are many other possible conclusions. Libet himself hoped that his results would defeat materialism. They did not do so, but nor did they prove that materialism is correct. Instead I think they served to reveal just how confused our thinking still is about consciousness and free will.

Indeed, what makes this all so extraordinary is why everyone was so surprised at Libet's results. Almost all scientists and most philosophers claim to be materialists (or at least not to be dualists). In other words, they ought to assume that the brain process would start the action, and not be at all surprised by the results. Yet they were surprised, and go on being surprised. I think the reason is that they, like most people, *feel* as though they consciously decide to act, and that their consciousness causes things to happen.

So here we have a simple clash between the physical and the mental; between how things are in the physical brain and how they feel from the inside. How do we resolve it?

I suspect that we will never do so without a revolution in the way we think about consciousness. I don't mean a revolution involving quantum physics, or telepathy, or new forces of nature, or other-worldly spirits and souls. I mean a revolution that goes deep down into our own minds and actually transforms our experience, so that we can talk and think in a different way. And this way would have to be something so counter-intuitive that it really does root out dualism.

These problems have left me doubting many of the assumptions that are commonly made in thinking about consciousness. The main ones are these:

There is something it is like to be me.
I am a persisting conscious entity.

I can consciously cause my own actions.

Consciousness is like a stream.

Seeing means having a rich and detailed movie in the brain.

Consciousness has unity both in one moment, and through time.

Brain activity can be either conscious or unconscious.

Consciousness has contents.

Experiences happen in the present moment, the now.

I doubt them because the scientific evidence suggests that at least some of them cannot be true. Is this doubt the same doubt as the Zen monk is supposed to arouse by contemplating a difficult koan? I think so. And that is one reason why I think meditation may help with the science of consciousness.

This is really the purpose of this book. We face a conflict between scientific findings and our own intuitions. Could common intuitions about consciousness be wrong? Many people would say they could not be; that they know exactly what their consciousness is like and no one can tell them otherwise; they know that they are a continuing conscious being who experiences a rich and vivid sensory world, that their conscious thoughts dictate their actions, and that of course they know what it's like to be them.

I question that last point. Perhaps I don't actually know what it's like to be me. Perhaps I have been making assumptions all along about how I feel, how I perceive, how I think, without looking carefully at all, and that's why consciousness seems to be such a mystery. So now I want to look into my own mind very carefully indeed, and see whether my uncritical assumptions about my own experience might conceivably have been wrong.

My garden shed

1

Am I conscious now?

O f course I am. Yes, I am conscious now.

Am I conscious now?

Of course I am. Yes, I am conscious now.

But something odd happened. When I asked myself the question it was as though I became conscious at that moment. Was I not conscious before? It felt as though I was waking up – coming to consciousness when I asked the question – because I asked the question.

What is going on? (Calm down. Take it slowly.) Am I conscious now?

I can remember what was happening just before I asked the question, so it seems that someone must have been conscious. Was someone else conscious a moment before – as though the waking up is a change in who is conscious? It certainly didn't feel as though it could have been me because I just woke up, but surely it wasn't anyone else, for who else could there be in here?

Another possibility is that I wasn't really conscious before I asked the question. This is deeply troubling. For I've never asked this question before. Surely I cannot have been unconscious, or semi-conscious, all my life, can I? Perhaps there are lots of things that make me conscious apart from asking this particular question. Even so, this is rather scary. It certainly seems as though I must spend a lot of my time unconscious, otherwise I could not have this definite sensation of coming awake when I ask 'Am I conscious now?'

Let me ask it again. Can I reproduce the awakening and look into it to see what it is really like?

Am I conscious now?

I practise it a lot, for weeks and months. I keep doing it. I keep asking 'Am I conscious now?' To begin with the hardest part is remembering to ask. But I want to know. I want to understand what it means to be conscious. So I persevere. Little things remind me of the question – a look, a sound, a sudden emotion – any of them can propel me into asking. And then it happens again and again; it feels as though I am waking up. Yes, of course I am conscious now. Yes of course I am, but I wasn't a moment ago.

I know now, from all the many students who have trodden this path with me, that the hardest part is remembering to ask the question. Even though I feel driven to keep asking, there are often long gaps when I fail to do it. So I've tried various strategies, and my students have too.

Some tell me they put stickers all over their house: 'Are you conscious?' on the front door; 'Am I conscious now?' on the toaster; 'Conscious?' on the kettle; 'Are you sure you're conscious now?' on the pillow. Others get into pairs so that they can keep reminding each other – 'Are you conscious now?' Some take to special times and places; they ask the question every time they go to the loo, or always ask the question when going to bed, or always remember when they have a drink or food. Sometimes these tricks work; sometimes they don't.

I wonder why it's so hard. It almost seems as though there is something conspiring to prevent us asking the question; some thickness in the way, some awful lethargy that makes it hard to face up to … to what? To being fully aware, I suppose. The question propels becoming conscious and becoming open to everything around. Although it seems impossible, in good faith, to answer 'No', it is hard work to answer 'Yes', 'Yes, I am conscious now', perhaps because it reminds me that most of the time I cannot have been. But it's worth it. I persevere.

Am I conscious now? Yes.

Ah, here's a new question: Can I stay this way?

A funny thing happens, again and again. I ask the question. I answer yes. I am fully conscious now, I have woken up to this present moment. Right. This is easy. Here I am. But before I know it I am far away in distraction, thinking about something else, being angry with someone, being miles away in the past or the future or something completely invented and troubling and annoying.

The question appears again (from where?). I sigh. Lost again. Yes, I am conscious now, but where was I? Forget that for a moment. Steady. Ask the question.

Am I conscious now? Yes.

It troubles me that I seem so often to be unconscious. I wonder what this unconsciousness is. I cannot believe I spend most of my life in a kind of darkness. Surely that cannot be so. Yet every time I ask this question it feels as though I am waking up, or that a light is switching on. All the more troubling is that this light is so rare. By asking the question and switching it on, I seem to have stumbled on the fact that my normal state of life is some horrible kind of gloom. Was this why I was so troubled; so ill at ease? Was this why I so often felt that nothing was real; that nothing was clear, as though something I couldn't place obscured the view and made my head swim?

I want to explore this darkness; this normal state if that is what it is. But that is impossible isn't it? How can I look into the darkness, when looking makes it light?

The psychologist William James tried this back in the 1880s. He likened the stream of consciousness to a bird's life; an alternation of flights and perchings. He tried to see the flights for what they are, but found he annihilated them in the process, like a snowflake crystal caught in a warm hand. 'The attempt at introspective analysis in these cases is in fact like seizing a spinning top to catch its motion, or trying to turn up the gas quickly enough to see how the darkness looks.'

'To see how the darkness looks.'

This is too difficult. I must leave it for another time. For now, at least, I have found a way to make the light. It is a simple question, 'Am I conscious now?'

How can a question work such magic? I wonder what it means to ask a question. Surely a tape recorder blurting out the question a hundred times a day would not have the experience of becoming awake. Would it? Would part of a brain? I suppose that there must be more to it than just saying the words. Indeed, sometimes I repeat them too often and they lose all meaning. They become just a chant; a mantra; a meaningless sequence of sounds. That is not asking the question. So what is? What does it mean to ask a question? Is there some magic in the inquisitive brain?

The closest I can get is to think of it as a gesture – a grand gesture towards the world. It is a kind of openness. Asking means being open for an answer. Asking means waiting to see. Asking means being there for whatever is not me. I ask. Am I conscious now?

As the years go by and I keep on asking the question, something changes. At first it is very jerky. Something reminds me to ask, and I ask. Suddenly I am awake. Here it goes again. Here I am, awake in this moment. Where was I before? Have I been in the dark so much? I am annoyed with myself – how could you be so dull, so fast asleep. Wake up! But I am already awake. I am asking the question. All this is uncomfortable.

Gradually the transition eases. Waking up becomes a little smoother. Indeed, each time is reminiscent of the last. It is almost as though being awake is always the same, or at least it has more in common with other moments of being awake than does the ordinary blurry, difficult-to-see, darkness. I keep on asking 'Am I conscious now?'

Something odd happens. A continuity begins to appear. Whereas at first the question was always isolated and almost a shock to attempt, now it comes more easily and I try to keep the question open once I've asked, and answered, it.

Is it possible to keep on asking the same question for a long time, I wonder. The logic is simple. Asking this question always gets the answer 'Yes'. So if I keep on asking it I should remain conscious as long as the question is alive, shouldn't I? I try, and as the years pass it becomes easier to keep the question open. No longer does a door quietly close, only to be wrenched open again in fury at having let it close unnoticed once again. Gradually, gradually it is possible to keep asking the question. The words aren't really necessary any more. Rather, there just seems to be a questioning attitude, an openness of mind. Am I conscious now? Yes, I am, keep on that way, and now, and now, and gently now.

What is this continuity? For that is what it seems like: that after asking the question so often and so deeply, being here seems more continuous, not broken up again and again. But is this a continuity of self? Continuity of the world? Continuity of consciousness? Words and theories may be getting in the way. I must look some more.

Above all, this feeling of continuity seems to be the consequence of asking this question. Long ago, when I was first practising mindfulness, I wondered whether awareness really does become more continuous with practice. It was a question that bothered me a lot, for the process, if process there was, seemed to be so slow. Nevertheless, changes happened, and this sense of being continuously here, now, became more common, more available, less of a shock, easier to relax into without being whisked away in distraction. Eventually I concluded that awareness does become more continuous with practice – it can just take a very long time. Yes, this now is carrying on. The last moment and this and now, they are not broken up. Here, now.

What is remarkable is how very hard this is. I don't know why, and I don't know what is going on in all this business of asking such a simple question, but I do know that it is getting at the very stuff that drives me to know.

This is at its heart. I sit down again and keep on asking. At last something stabilises. The mind is calm enough to really look into this simplest of simple questions. I look.

I am in my garden hut, wrapped in blankets. It's mid-winter and very cold. I have sat for some time and the daylight is fading, and now I ask the familiar question.

Am I conscious now? Yes I am.

But did I say 'now'? When is this now? The only way to find out is to look. So I look some more. But this proves not to be easy, even though the present moment has stabilised.

At first it seems that obviously there is a now. This is when everything is happening. What is happening? This. And then this.

I had supposed there was some kind of sliding moment: the present moment, that glided along, marking the difference between the things that have already happened and the things yet to come; a boundary between the future and the past. But somehow this just does not accord with reality. I have read, in the literature on 'phenomenology', that there is a now, a 'just-past', and an immediate future. But this does not accord with reality either. I keep steady and look.

There's stuff all right. But is it happening now? I cannot see. It is blurry and indistinct. It is hard and painful to look. I cannot see. Everything that happens seems somehow to be spread out over time. There goes a flock of birds passing across my view. I hear a siren in the distance, ambulance, police car, fire engine, something passing along a road far away. But it takes time to be what it is. I cannot find its now.

Right. I can grab a now. I can grasp out with my attention. This, and this. They happened at once, didn't they. It was a now, I am sure, even though it is gone by the time I can have that certainty.

So it seems easy enough to create a now. I can grasp two things or several things, and bind them into a moment at once. But does that count? Am I not just making up a now? I want to find the now as it naturally is. This eludes me.

I ask again: Am I conscious now? and watch as the continuous now does whatever continuous nows do. There seems to be a choice – grasp at some of the things that are going on and bind them into a now – snap. That was it. That was a now-past now. Or else just let the myriad things keep doing whatever they are doing.

Then it seems clear. They are happening all right, as the continuity carries on. There is the flickering of the candle-light across the rough wooden floor, the spattering of rain on the roof above, and the blinking of distant lights scarcely seen, but none is precisely before or after the other – unless I grab them, bind them together and decide which came first. Indeed I really cannot say when any of them is happening. The best I can say is that they arise and are gone.

This is troubling. It is one thing to say there is no now but another to understand what that might mean. I struggle to work out why this would be a problem, and become confused. I am so used to thinking about past, present and future that I cannot work out what it would mean for there to be no now. And yet there does not seem to be a now. What counts as now seems to depend on which way I tackle things. When I sit quietly, doing nothing, there is no obvious choice of what is now. Stuff just happens.

I sit. Am I conscious now?

Years pass.

Am I conscious now? No I'm not.

What?

I realise for the first time that I can answer 'No'. What if this slippery, difficult, not quite being really here, is not being conscious, and I should have been answering 'no' all along?

Is this the same as looking into the darkness?

Is there any light?

2

What was I conscious of a moment ago?

If I become conscious only when I ask whether I am, then what about just before I asked? I seem to remember what was happening a moment ago, but was I conscious of it at the time? Can I look back and find out what I was conscious of a moment before I asked?

This reminds me of a familiar enough experience. It goes like this. I am reading, or writing, or doing something else, when suddenly I notice that the clock is chiming. I have only just noticed it, yet it seems as though I have been hearing it all along because I can easily count backwards and know that it has sounded three times already. I go on counting. It strikes six.

Was I conscious of the first strike? Apparently not; otherwise I wouldn't have had that very odd sensation of suddenly becoming aware of the fourth strike and of recalling the previous three. But if I wasn't conscious of it at the time, how come I can remember the sound so clearly in my mind's ear? Was it unconscious at the time the clock struck and then became conscious later? What could this mean?

I decide to investigate.

I sit still, in my hut, and calm the mind. My plan is simple. I am going to wait until all is calm and then ask 'What was I conscious of a moment ago?' It's calm.

I ask.

I am conscious of the wooden floor of my hut; I've been looking at it for a while. What else? I listen out. Of course – there is the sound of our cat purring by my side. I have been listening to her for a while now, or so it seems. I can remember that purring going back in time. I have been listening, haven't I? Well, maybe. Yet when I suddenly thought of the purring it was as though it came into my consciousness right then, just as the clock's chime had done. So – was I conscious of it a moment ago or not? Surely there must be an answer, mustn't there?

I try again, still sitting here, my eyes resting on the floor; the damp garden spread out in front of me. I look back with an open mind, still here now but asking the question. What was I conscious of a moment ago?

What about my own body? I can feel my seat on the wooden stool. I can feel my hands held together in my lap. And there's that slight ache in my left knee. That ache has been going on for a long time. I know it has. I can look back into the continuous dull, slight pain and feel that it has. And there's more. With exasperated shock I recognise there's a siren sounding – out there in the road. It's loud and obvious. Why didn't I realise it instantly? That noise has been going on for about three or four loud swoops – nah nah, nah nah. I was conscious of it then wasn't I? Was I?

No, I wasn't. Or at least, I am not sure. It took me several tries at the question to hit upon that sound, and when I did it was loud and obvious and had been going on for some time. But what if I hadn't been searching? Would I have been conscious of the noise at the time and then forgotten it? Or would I never have become conscious of it at all? Would that vivid sound have disappeared without trace? It did seem vivid. It did feel as though I had been consciously listening to those three or four howls. Had I?

Was I conscious of the sound a moment ago, or not?

Surely there must be an answer, mustn't there? I'm reminded of Dan Dennett's challenging contrast between Orwellian and Stalinesque revisions.

According to Dennett, it's natural to assume that there must be a true answer to the question 'What was I conscious of at some particular time?' So it must either be true that I was conscious of only the floor and my hands and the ache, or true that I was conscious of the siren as well. We cannot imagine that there might be no right answer.

To show why we could be wrong, he invents two ways of describing what happened when I suddenly became aware of the siren. In one version, I wasn't aware of the siren at the time but, when I asked the question, something like Orwell's Ministry of Truth rewrote the past, pulling out a previously unconscious memory and making it seem as though I'd been conscious of the siren all along. In the other version I *was* conscious of the siren at the time, and the question just alerted me to the fact. If I hadn't asked the question the memory would have faded away and I might later have been like a witness at one of Stalin's show trials, firmly declaring that I never heard the siren at all. So which is right? Was I really conscious of the siren or not?

There is no answer, says Dennett. There is simply no way in which one could ever tell. Looking inside the brain won't tell you, for the signals were being processed in the relevant bits of brain whichever way you describe it, and asking the person won't tell you because she doesn't know either. So it's a difference that makes no difference. And what should we do with a difference that makes no difference? Forget it; accept that there is no answer to the question 'What was I conscious of a moment ago?' Can that really be right?

This question is proving interesting, and difficult. I resolve to pursue it night and day. I have a go – asking myself from time to time, in the midst of ordinary life, 'What was I conscious of a moment ago?'

As I get used to the exercise, the response settles down to a pattern. I usually find several things; several candidates for things I might have been conscious of a moment ago. Sounds are the easiest bet. They hang on. They take time. When I light upon them, they always seem to have been going on for some time, and it feels as though I have been conscious of them. There is the sound of the cars outside in the distance. There's the ticking of the clock. There's the beating of my own heart. And then – oh goodness me – how could I have ignored that. There's my breath. Surely I have been watching my breath, haven't I?

I have never practised watching the breath as a formal meditation practice, but the breath is always there. When I sit, it goes slowly in and out, settling down and becoming deep and slow. I know that. I have been watching it haven't I? Yes? No? Have I? How come I don't know?

Let's get this clear. After many other threads of past awarenesses I lit upon the breath. More than any other experience, it seemed to have been going on and on. More than that, it seemed as though 'I' had been watching this breath going in and out. So I must have been conscious of it. And yet I wasn't. I mean, it took a deliberate act of casting around for things I might not have noticed, to find this one. I was concentrating on that patch of wall, wasn't I? Was I watching the breath as well? They seem to have nothing to do with each other. It is as though I only brought them together by asking the question. I asked the question 'What was I conscious of a moment ago?' and by way of answer these two disparate threads of experience came up. It seemed that I was conscious of both and yet the two seemed to have been completely separate – far apart.

Stop. Think. This is very odd. Do it all again. And again. And again. I find the same thing, many times. There are always more threads to be found out there; threads of what I seem to have been conscious of but which seem to have had nothing to do with each other. This is the oddest thing, although it seems rather obvious now: whenever I ask the question 'What am I conscious of now?' there is only one answer – this. But when I ask the question 'What was I conscious of a moment ago?' there are several answers.

What's going on?

I practise again and again. I ask the question walking along, when working at my desk, when digging in the garden, when in conversation. Always the same thing seems to happen. There's something I'm paying attention to; the salad I'm making, the earth on my spade, the words I'm listening to. And then, when I look, I can find at least one, and often many, threads of things that I might have been conscious of a moment ago but which seem to have had no connection with each other.

Who then was conscious of them? Surely someone was because they have that quality of having been listened to, having been stared at, having been felt or smelt or tasted – by someone. Was it me? Unless there were several mes at once, then no. Or is it that I am split up in reverse; that going backwards I can find lots of routes to the past? This is how it seems. Threads is the right word. From any point – from any now – I can look back and find these myriad threads. They feel perfectly real. They feel as though I was listening to that blackbird's song, that drone of traffic, that distant hammering somewhere up the hill, the purring cat beside me. But each one has this peculiar quality.

Perhaps it will help to take one and analyse it carefully.

I take that screech of the crow as it flew overhead. I heard it, yes, but what happened was this. I was sitting there, in my hut, watching the floor, feeling my breathing, aware of the row of plants beyond the door and of the damp stones between me and them, when suddenly I realised that I had just heard this almighty screech. A crow had swooped close overhead and cried out 'EEEEEuchhhhhh'. It must have been half a second ago.

I wasn't expecting it. I wasn't aware of it instantly. It took some time to penetrate. And then 'EEEEEuchhhhhh'. I knew I'd heard it, but it was already past. So ...

Here is the difficulty. The sound happened, and then half a second later I became aware that it had already happened. So I naturally want to ask whether I was, or was not, conscious of the crow at the time it shrieked. No. At the time I wasn't. I know that because the first thing I knew was having heard it. The screech was already just past and I remembered having heard it. Ah. So this was a memory – not the real thing. I wasn't conscious of it at the time it really happened; I only became conscious of it by remembering it afterwards.

Is this right? If I am to pursue this line of inquiry I must be able to distinguish things I am really conscious of now from ones that I only remember being conscious of after they have passed. And I know this will not do. The harder I look, the less obviously I can tell the difference. The two seemed so obviously different at first, but now I'm no longer sure. Is there a right answer?

I must check. I try out a few more examples. I can cast my mind around and hear that rumble of a lorry going up the hill. Was I conscious of it before I looked for it? Ah – there's an insect crawling on my arm. I can feel that it's been progressing upwards from my right elbow for some time now. But was I actually conscious of it before I looked around for another example? Or not?

I've been listening to a blackbird's song. I pay it more attention and try to listen to it right *now* as it is happening, to stay with it. With dismay I realise that songs take time. I cannot recognise the song as a song, or the bird as a blackbird, until at least a few notes have passed. So was I conscious of the structure of that beautiful song as it unfolded or did I become conscious of its beauty only once I'd heard enough to appreciate its shape? When did the consciousness itself happen? Surely there must be an answer mustn't there?

The problem seems just as bad whether I consider all those multiple threads that I can remember and cannot tell which I was conscious of, or whether I just consider one at a time and ask when it came into my consciousness. I simply cannot tell. And if I cannot tell, who can?

I like to fantasise that someone could look inside my brain and tell me the answer; that they could point some clever machine at my head and tell me definitely when the sound, or touch, or feel, reached my consciousness, but is there such a place? Certainly scientists could put electrodes on my scalp and watch the waves of activity dancing over different areas, or put me in a scanner and watch the neural activity as it surges in through the thalamus, to the sensory cortex and on to other areas of the brain. They could probably tell me a lot about what I was hearing and seeing and even thinking about, but they would not be able to say 'Yes, this sound or thought was *conscious*, and this one was not.' Why not? Because they don't know what to look for. All brain cells work in much the same way, and no one has yet found a special place where consciousness happens, or a special process uniquely correlated with conscious, as opposed to unconscious, events.

Will they ever? Many neuroscientists think so, and are hunting for the 'neural correlates of consciousness' to find it. They are looking for a certain part of the brain, or a particular process, which reliably correlates with conscious as opposed to unconscious processes. This is something of a Holy Grail for consciousness studies. But if I don't know which sights and sounds I was conscious of, and which I was not, and I cannot tell anyone else which I was conscious of, then no one can possibly know, and so this whole line of scientific research must be entirely misguided.

I take stock. At any moment I can trace back various threads into the past. Each of them is something that I seem to have been conscious of for some time, and yet each of them seems only to have popped into my consciousness when I went searching for it by asking the question. I cannot say I was conscious of all of them because they seemed to come to light only when I looked for them. And each one seems, in looking back, to be quite disconnected from the others. I don't want to say that different mes were conscious of them because I thought there was only one me. I don't want to say that I was unconscious of them until I pulled them into my consciousness because then I have to distinguish conscious-now experiences from consciously remembered experiences, and that I cannot do. I am stuck.

How can I get out of this impasse. Perhaps then, I muse, the trouble is caused by the way I'm looking back. Perhaps I am just concocting fantasies about what I might have been listening to. I know that once I latch onto one of these threads it can seem awfully real, as though it stretches back and back and back. Perhaps instead I should stop pulling on imaginary threads and try to catch the whole thing – catch what I was really conscious of just a moment ago.

Time to calm the mind again. Take a clear, calm, spacious mind, and look; settle in, calm down, become still and then pop the question 'What was I conscious of a moment ago?'

I settle down. The myriad things appear and disappear. I pay attention to everything and nothing. I choose nothing above anything else; the mind gently alights on this and that, and lets go again. Nothing lasts. Things flow. Events come and go. Now.

What was I conscious of a moment ago?

I stop. I haven't a clue. I don't know. I really don't know.

But if I don't know who does?

Something truly terrible is here. There is no past. I have absolutely no idea what went before this.

Oh yes, I can grasp at threads. I can concoct all those threads of listening, hearing, feeling and touching. But what if I don't? What if I just stop and ask 'What was I conscious of a moment ago?' Nothing but a void. There is nothing there.

I'm too scared to look straight into the void. It is not a blackness, nor any perceptible absence of anything. It just isn't.

Surely I dare. Yes I do. I will look. I will look in spite of the fear.

Yet the appearance of this void is fleeting. It came as an instant and was washed away by clinging onto some new present thing. I must look again. I get a sense of a layer or film or imperceptible boundary from which this present moment is continuously appearing, but I cannot grasp or see it clearly. Something out of nothing. How can all this come out of nothing?

3

Who is asking the question?

Who is asking the question? What does that mean? This makes no sense. Which question? This question of course. The who in the question. Help. Stop.

I get the impression that if I could really hurl myself into this impossible question then … then what? I don't know. I'll start again, calm down, and try an easier tack.

Who is asking the question? I am. I am sitting here looking at the wet flagstones outside my hut. Let me investigate this instead. Who is looking at the stone? This is easier. I can see the stone over there, flat and grey with ups and downs and puddles where the rain collects, and wet leaves stuck here and there. Now who is seeing all this? There is no escaping the flagstone. There it is. And there is no escaping the fact that I am looking from over here. There is perspective: a viewpoint. Were I to look from somewhere else it would look different. Were someone else looking from over there they would see it in a different way. From here it looks like this. Right – so now I can draw a line between there and here. Over there is the flagstone. Over here is me. And who is this?

I look. I turn the looking inwards, from pointing out there at the stone to pointing in here at what is looking at the stone. What?

I find nothing. I cannot grasp it. I know there must be something here. It is me, isn't it? But it seems to elude me every way I look. I try again, going back to a calm mind with a steady gaze. I ask again. Who is looking? Again I find nothing.

I get cross. Surely it must be possible to find out what is looking. I keep trying. The flagstone is there. The direction and perspective are there. Something must be at this end – looking. But still I cannot find it. And who is trying to find it? Is this seeker the same me as the one who is looking at the stone or … Something is wrong here. Try again. Settle down and watch.

The world arises. Here it is. The distant traffic thrums on. The rain is dripping from the roof onto the stones with a steady patter. The plants are there, and their reflection shimmers in the scrap of puddle. There are all the threads that seem to have been going on. There they are; trolling along as ever. Let them be. There is a stillness at the centre of all this stuff. Eventually the question pops up again. Who is asking the question?

I don't know. I can't tackle it. It is too difficult. I feel stupid and blind.

I'll try another tack.

Here is all this world, all these threads, all this stuff. Who is watching them? This must be a sensible question, mustn't it? After all, there are a lot of experiences right here and now, so there must be someone experiencing them, mustn't there? That is how it seems. So all I have to do is to let the experiences be and then pop the question. Who is experiencing them? Perhaps this will be the same me as in the question 'Who is asking the question?' Then I'll know.

I look. Here is all this stuff. It seems to be out there some-where, and I seem to be in here looking out at it all. Let's forget the sounds and stick with vision for a moment; I'll try to work with that. Here I am sitting in here and looking out at the garden with its plants and trees and the garage roof and the distant buildings. Now, if they are out there, and I am in here, then there must be a boundary, or edge, or divide, between them and me. If I could just look for the edge I might then be able to flip from looking from the inside out, to looking from the outside in.

So where is this boundary between the world out there and me in here? I see a twist of hair, hanging between me and it. Is this the edge? Am I this side of the hair and the experiences the other? No. That's silly. I must work harder and more carefully. Let's start again at the flagstone. There it is. Now I want to work gradually inwards until I find the edge and then flip over from seeing the world out there to seeing the me in here. Right. Go.

There's the stone with its puddles and dirt and leaves and reflec-tions. Here, a little nearer, is the step and the wooden floor of my hut. It merges into the rug at my feet and that merges, oddly enough, into my own legs. I know these legs belong to my body, but I'm still looking at them from over here. So they are still outside of the me who's looking. Carry on, carefully now. Coming a little closer and now a little vaguer, I glimpse my folded hands and the rough muddle of a woolly jumper around my neck. Getting close. Is this all? A hint of see-through edge of nose and that twist of hair. This must be it. What comes next after the edge and that hair? Here we go …

I have it! Here it is! Inwards from there is … It's the garden again. Damn. Here is the stone again, and the floor and the drips and the plants. I can go round and round, starting with the middle of the view out there, working in carefully towards myself in the centre, and there I find only the same old view, to start all over again. How did that happen? I was looking for the me that was looking and I found only the world.

It's a familiar enough trick, but easily forgotten. Look for the viewing self and find only the view. I am, it seems, the world I see.

I remember the first time this happened to me, many years ago, walking with a group of Buddhists in the Mendip hills near my home. A friend started talking about Douglas Harding's book *On Having No Head* and, surprised to learn that I'd never even heard of it, introduced me to the idea.

We were standing at the edge of a field, looking out across a wooded valley and over fields full of sheep to the hills beyond.

'Point at that hill', he said, 'and concentrate on what you can see there.' I pointed and concentrated.

'Now come a little closer and point at your feet', he said, 'and concentrate on what you see there.' I pointed and concentrated.

'Point at your tummy', he said, 'and concentrate on what you see there.' I pointed and concentrated.

'Move up to your chest', he said, 'and concentrate on what you see there.' I pointed and concentrated.

'Now point straight between your eyes', he said. I pointed and …

No. Scream. What? Eeeeeek. I found the finger pointing and …

I had no head. There was my body all right, with its visible feet, legs, tummy, chest and then what? Of course I know I have a head. I can touch it and see it in the mirror, but I'd never noticed that I can't see it myself, directly; that all my life I've been walking around without a visible head. I laughed happily. On top of this headless body seemed to be the whole world of friends, and grass, and trees and hills. I'd lost my head and gained the world. I guess it's always like that. How odd never to have noticed before.

Once you've seen it, the 'Headless Way' is still easy to lose, and I'm afraid to say I simply lost it again. I didn't know how to practise, and I let the new vision slip away, although I remembered it intellectually. Then, many years later, a similar vision returned, though now in a completely different way.

It was a lovely spring day and Adam, my partner, and I went out into the garden for our morning meditation. We sat looking gently down at the lawn, facing towards a big flower bed full of powder blue forget-me-nots, with little specks of yellow and white. I paid open attention to everything I could see and hear, and in the space at the top of my shoulders I found no head, only forget-me-nots. I looked for the self who was looking at the forget-me-nots, and simply became them. It was very simple; very obvious.

What is not obvious is how to take this view into the rest of life. I fear I have been rather feeble in this. Nevertheless I did begin to practise looking at everything this way. Everything that comes up – that is where my head should be; that is what I am right now. This view from the window; I am that. This desk and computer; I am that. This table laid for dinner; I am that. Some things are easy; some are not. Sitting quietly at home is easy, going out into town is not.

The hardest is other people. There's some stupid bastard doing a U-turn in the middle of the road right in front of my bike. I am angry and want to shout 'You idiot – what do you think you're doing? You nearly knocked me off!' Can the sight of that idiotic man be me? Yes. Of course. If I stop, calm down, and search for the me who is looking at him I will find only him, and his car, and the road. If I search for the me who is angry with him I will find only the anger bubbling up.

It's the same with everything I experience; there is not a separate me as well as the experience. It is hard to accept that I am all those people walking down the street; that I am, at least in this fleeting moment, that Muslim woman with her stupid veil, that annoying child with the ice cream, that crowd of giggling school girls. Yet somehow or another this way of looking makes it easier to be kind.

But all that is long ago and I am evading the question again.

Who is asking the question? This is still too difficult. It is one step to see that the perceiving self is none other than the perceived world, but it is much harder to stare straight into this impossible, self-referential, daft question: Who is asking the question?

Asking. Asking? This is a kind of doing. Perhaps I can creep up on it through other kinds of action. After all, when I think about myself I think of myself as an actor; I am the one who acts;

I am the one who decides to do things and then does them. When I am washing up then there is a me who is doing it. When I am working there is a me who is making the effort. Perhaps I can look into this me, and so find out who is asking the question.

It happens today that I am polishing a set of brass bells, from a tiny, tinkling hand bell to a large fire engine's bell. I like to break the long day of meditation with a session of work: something physical that stirs up the muscles and keeps me awake. I would do some weeding or digging, but today it's been pouring with rain all day, so I set to work on the bells instead. I pull out a wad of Brasso from its familiar tin, with its characteristic smell and horrible rough feel on my hands. I rub the wet stuff on. I scrub the brass steadily, up and down, up and down, up and down, firmly clutching the wad of dirty fibres. I see the arms in front of me, coming out of nowhere. Who is polishing the bells?

I think of Hui Neng, the Sixth Patriarch of Chan, and his famous poem. It's one of my favourite Zen stories. When Hui Neng was a lowly monk, cleaning rice in the kitchen for months on end, the head of the monastery, the ageing fifth Patriarch, put out a competition to find the monk who would be chosen to suceed him as Patriarch; he would give the robe and bowl to whoever showed their understanding of the essence of mind by writing the best poem.

The chief monk, whom everyone thought was bound to succeed, wrote something like this:

> The body is the wisdom tree,
> The mind a stand with mirror bright.
> Take care to clean it all the time
> And let no dust alight.

The fifth Patriarch knew that this poem showed no true insight but he told all the other monks to learn it off by heart all the same. Then Hui Neng, who could neither read nor write, heard the other monks chanting the poem and so made up his own response, persuading someone else to write it for him on the monastery wall:

> There is no wisdom tree
> No stand with mirror bright.
> Since all is empty from the start
> Where could the dust alight?

The Patriarch immediately recognised Hui Neng's understanding and, knowing that the other monks would be jealous, summoned him at night, secretly gave him the master's robe and bowl, and told him to go quickly and escape.

My shiny brass bell is all new and bright now. Is this the mind? Polished and bright? Who is polishing?

There are the arms all right. They move up and down, the brass appears and disappears. The threads of distant traffic go their way. The boiler hums in the background and the light is coming in through the window. I look upwards along the arms. I have this awful suspicion that I know what I will find. Indeed. The arms just fade out of sight at the top. There is nothing here. The arms are rubbing the brass and the arms come out of nothing at all. There is nowhere for the dust to alight.

Who is polishing? Who is asking 'Who is polishing?'? Keep polishing. Keep asking.

It is time to put the bells down and go back to meditation. Sitting again my breath comes out; in and out, in and out, steam in the cold damp air. Where is it coming from? Absolutely nowhere. There is a vast void here – where I thought was my inside. The breath just comes and dissipates into the air, and then again, out of nowhere. How could I not have noticed this vast nothingness before, when it is all pervasive and apparently always here? Who knows. Best, I think, just to sit with it. After all, I'm not getting anywhere with what I'm meant to be doing. I'm meant to be asking the question 'Who is asking the question?'

It's too difficult. I don't know.

Well?

Who …?

4

Where is this?

Where is this? Where is what?

Well I have to start somewhere, so how about starting with what is right in front of me, here and now. It is winter in my hut, and right in front of me are three sprigs of bright yellow winter jasmine. My gaze is resting gently on them. There they are: yellow, bright, clear. Where is this yellow winter jasmine then?

Sit; look. I look steadily and calmly at the flowers.

I have a feeling that this question is going to prove more tricky than it appears. It seems to me pretty obvious that the flowers are there, in front of me, where they seem to be, but I sense something wrong. I must explore a bit further. In fact there seem to be two obvious answers and I will try them both; the flowers are out there in front of me where they seem to be, or they are inside my head.

One answer at a time, I will have a go.

What is wrong with the idea that the yellow flowers are right there, where they seem to be, about two feet in front of my face? Actually quite a lot, now I come to think of it. Philosophers have argued for centuries over the location of experiences – are they in the brain that creates them, in the outside world where they seem to be, or without any location at all, as Descartes believed? Psychologist, Max Velmans, builds his entire theory of 'reflexive monism' on this question. He claims that the contents of consciousness are not exclusively in the brain but also in the perceived physical world, but few believe he has escaped from dualism by this route.

There are lots of problems. I'll work them through as I sit very still, with the flowers before me.

I realise I have made some kind of object out of the flowers, as though it is independent of my experience. But the question was 'Where is this?' and 'this' is my experience of the flowers. I am seeing them from over here, and from here they appear in a particular way. This petal overlaps that one, these stalks go in just that pleasing pattern across each other; that whole shape is just as it is. I know that if I moved they would appear differently. Someone else would see them from a different angle. The trouble is that I am imagining an abstract three-dimensional space and putting these actual flowers into their position. There's nothing wrong with that. If I wanted to measure them, or paint them, I could use that abstract construction to work out the coordinates of every point in the whole complicated bunch. But that abstraction would not be 'this'. 'This' is my experience of the flowers right now. And the question is 'Where is this?'

How about tackling the colour. That might be simpler. This wonderful bright, special, only-winter-jasmine-can-be-like-that yellow is right here in front of me. Where is this?

I let go, calm down, and look. The yellow is unsteady. The more I try to capture what it's like now, the less steady it seems.

But it's still there, and yellow all right. Perhaps I am trying too hard, and chasing the yellow away.

Just sit and let it be, until I'm ready to start again.

Here is the yellow, bright and clear.

I take the two obvious answers. The first is that the yellow is out there, on the petals of the flower, right where it seems to be. This is a no hoper. I know that. Here is the problem. The colour yellow is not really in the flowers at all because it only appears to be yellow when a particular sort of visual system looks at it. If a bee flew over that flower now, for example, it would not perceive it as yellow like I do. Bees have visual systems quite unlike ours, with compound eyes made of lots of little eyes instead of just two big eyes with lenses. And although bees cannot see some of the red colours we can see, they can see far further into the ultraviolet than we can. All this has evolved because many flowers use bees to pollinate them. Over millions of years, flowers attractive to bees were better pollinated and produced more offspring than unattractive ones; bees that could detect the colours better got more nectar from the flowers and so produced more offspring able to detect them. So the insects' visual systems and the colours of flowers evolved together. There are probably guide marks on the petals that I cannot see and the bee can, because they are only visible in the ultraviolet. The yellow, then, is not out there where it seems to be, in the petals of my beautiful flower. It takes me, and my particular eyes, and my particular brain, as well as the flowers, to make this yellow.

Hmm. Let's try the other tack. The yellow is in my head.

I know something about that too, and it doesn't help. When I look at a yellow flower the colour receptors in the back of my eye start firing with electrical bursts, and send signals along the optic nerve to my brain. Because the flower is yellow some nerve cells fire more than others, and this information is carried on to the visual areas at the back of the cortex. There, in areas called V1, V2, V4 and so on, there is more firing of certain groups of nerve cells and less of others. If I were looking at a purple flower, the proportions firing would be correspondingly reversed. So if neuroscientists could look inside my brain in enough detail, they would probably be able to tell which colour I was looking at.

But is this neural activity the yellow itself? How can it be? One neuron firing is much like another. Channels in the membranes open and close; sodium ions and calcium ions flow in and out, waves of depolarisation flow along the fibres. All neurons work much the same way, even though they are connected up in such fantastically complicated patterns. Where is the yellow in the yellow-firing cells?

It is not surprising that we have no satisfactory science of consciousness. The experience of yellow seems to be left out of our rapidly improving descriptions of how the brain works. Something is horribly wrong. But what?

I am stuck. That yellow. It is so … yellow. This is how it is, but 'Where is this?'

It's time for a break. I get up stiffly, wriggle my legs, pull on my waterproof top, and set off running round the garden; up and down the paths, up and down the steps to the garage, round and round the vegetable patch. I don't look up, but watch the ground in front of me so as not to disturb the meditation. Blurs of grey stone, and green grass pass as I run.

I feel a smile forming, though whether of delight or despair I do not know. Colours are the quintessential philosopher's qualia; those supposedly basic, private, indescribable, raw feels that make up all our experiences; the 'what it's like' of subjective experience; the awfulness of pain or the redness of red. This is what a science of consciousness is supposed to explain; how can the objective workings of a brain give rise to these qualia?

Philosopher Paul Churchland is sure that the redness of red simply *is* the patterns of firing within our brain. He says that just as most people now happily accept that light *is* electromagnetic waves, so in the future people will happily accept that their experience of red is a particular sort of brain activity. Others think we need a revolution in science to explain qualia, such as quantum computing in tiny parts of brain cells, though how this helps I cannot imagine. More radically, Dan Dennett rejects the entire concept of qualia, along with the 'actual phenomenology', the what it's like now. There's no such thing, he says. There are no simple, basic, private raw feels that need to be explained.

No such thing as what this is really like?

Well, is there? I slow down, the passing grass slows down. It's green. What is this greenness of green? It's like. Um.

Settle down again. In my hut I slowly, slowly light another incense stick, paying attention and moving with care. Calm the mind again and look. The rain is easing and the yellow flowers are where they were before.

There's something very obvious here. I began by separating out those lovely yellow flowers from everything around. I lost 'this' altogether. 'This' is the whole thing; the whole experience; this.

All around is the hut and the garden beyond; and beyond that the city with its droning cars and distant sirens and thumping of some machine. All this comes and goes, waxes and wanes. The flowers are there in the midst of it all. So, Where is this? I run through that now familiar route. My eyes rest gently on the flowers as I mentally traverse the space between them and me. There's the step, there's the floor, there are my knees – getting hazy now – there is the rug and my hands hardly perceptible – merging into … what? Right where I thought I should be, here are the yellow flowers. Here they are again. And me? Only a nameless void, filled with the yellow flowers.

A petal drops.

It is night time in my hut. A candle sputters somewhere behind me. I look up. Most things I ignore when I'm meditating but I need to know that the candle isn't going to burn the place down. I look up in front of me. I see the reflection of the candle in the window, sputtering a little, flickering back and forth. There are two of them; candles hanging in their glass globes. In the window I see their reflections, back and forth, one directly, another from behind, this one reflected twice in both the windows, the other three times, another (I lose track of which) five or ten times, reaching out in an ever diminishing flow. Where are they? Are they in front or behind? Do I see the candles? Their reflections? An image in the glass? An image projected into the space beyond? Where is this?

I have no idea. The rows of lights pass right through me, or pass through what I once thought was me, or where I once thought I must be sitting. Where is this?

There are many things that happen all at once, or separately, or in their several threads. The rain spatters on the roof in a steady drum. Odd drips fall onto something loud, somehow separate from the rain. Oh – and there's that perpetual traffic sound that someone seems to have been listening to all this while. And a late bird is still chirruping somewhere. All around is the space of the hut, and the matting clearly there in vision, and the cold of the damp air. Where is this?

Suddenly a plane bursts overhead; a roaring, loud, insistent, violent noise. I can see it in my mind. It is huge and metal with great big wings. There are engines throwing out hot air and vapour trails. There are rows of seats with people in them and stewards and a pilot and carpets and …

Once, long ago, I had a strange experience with an aeroplane. It was on retreat in Wales, nearly twenty years ago. We had been told to go outside for one session and sit up on the mountainside. We were to look at the ground before us for about twenty minutes or so and then look up at the valley or the trees or whatever was there. I sat for twenty minutes or so. I looked up, and just then a plane roared overhead. I saw the plane in my mind's eye. I saw the rows of seats, the people, the trays of airline food, imagining them involuntarily as they passed overhead. It was so loud. It was fearfully loud.

Suddenly I realised I was wrong. The noise was in fact a military plane; they often do exercises over the Welsh mountains. So it was nothing like the one I had imagined after all. So what was I hearing? I didn't know. I had no idea whether I was hearing a plane, that plane, any plane. There was a loud, deafening roar. My whole body shook with the screeching noise. But what was it. Where was I?

The whole world burst apart, and with it planes and trees, the valley and the cushion on which I sat, and me. I knew enough, even then, just to keep sitting. Later I walked down the hill again to join the others for tea. There they were. I saw their feet, my gaze down as usual, as I passed them or they passed me by. They were transparent. They were ghosts. There and not there. So was this ghost.

I sit here in my hut all these years later. It never happened again quite like that. Perhaps it never does. But the planes go by. Are they up there in the sky? This great roaring noise. Where is this?

My investigations haven't got me very far. I settle down to watch and ask. Where is this? This? I realise I have no idea what I am talking about. For I omitted to ask the simplest question at the beginning. Which 'this' am I supposed to be asking about? There's 'this', and now there's 'this'. And there are all those threads, going on their ways and seeming to stretch backwards into some indeterminate past. Someone seems to have been watching that breathing – slow and steady, clouds of visible breath coming out of nowhere and disappearing again into the invisible air. Someone was hearing that call of the blackbird in the tree, now, and again now. This bird or that? Breathe in and out. Which is this? Where is this?

5

How does thought arise?

This question is not one I set for myself, but one that took hold of me on a retreat at Maenllwyd in March 1993. The question itself was embedded in a series of questions, and these were embedded in a yet longer series of exercises. Though I struggled with them, I loved these questions, and returned to them on later formal retreats, on a solitary retreat at Maenllwyd, and finally at home in the winter of 2007 in my shed in the garden. I describe here just the first (now fifteen years ago) and the last of these attempts.

Called 'Introducing Tantra to the Path', this retreat was not one of John's usual Western Zen or Chan retreats, but was intended for Zen practitioners to get a taste of a different approach, one derived from Tibetan Buddhism rather than Chinese or Japanese Buddhism. The five days of structured meditation were based on a notebook compiled by a Tibetan master and brought back from India by John himself some years before.

The story of the notebook's discovery is itself extraordinary. In 1981 John was travelling in the Himalayas with a young anthropology student, in search of information for their study of the social history of Ladakh. One day they came across a lama called Khamtag Rimpoche, a Tibetan refugee, who invited them to drink beer with him, and questioned them closely on their reasons for being there and their practice of meditation. As they were leaving, he told them that he had a small monastery in the mountains where no one lived and that they would both be most welcome there. But he left without giving any instructions on how to find it.

John was impressed with this man and, feeling that he had been in the presence of 'one who knew', was determined to find him again. So, later that summer he set off to try to find the place, on a journey that became a pilgrimage in itself. Eventually a nun guided him and his young companion up a remote mountain, climbing dried-up waterfalls, and through a 400 foot limestone cleft only a few feet wide, finally emerging into a wide pasture ringed by snow-capped mountains. In the middle of this pasture lay a tiny – and deserted – monastery. Rather than leave immediately they waited, and waited. Then suddenly, after several days, the Rimpoche arrived, invited them in, and entertained them to a meal with liberal amounts of chang (the local beer) and arrack (strong spirit). As the drunken night wore on, the Rimpoche revealed much of his past training and accomplishment, and eventually produced a tattered notebook – one of only three copies of the Mahamudra instructions of his master Tipun Padma Chogyal. He asked the visitors to photograph the whole book and take it back with them to the West.

This was quite a responsibility. Mahamudra (or the 'great seal') is part of the deepest teachings of Tibetan Buddhism and such texts would traditionally have been kept secret, to be shared only with advanced students. Yet the lama knew that the old traditions were under threat and that John might be able to preserve the text. When morning came, and the drink wore off, he still insisted, and so it was that John photographed the notebook, had it translated, based several retreats on it and eventually had it published.

On the first day of our retreat, as we all sat round the hall on our cushions, John told us this story, and entrusted us with a few photocopied pages from 'Tipun's notebook'. But we were not to read them yet. First we had to calm the mind.

The first day was horrible. At 5.30 a.m. someone banged together two pieces of wood, the usual rising signal at Maenllwyd, and we had to be dressed and outside within ten minutes. There, in the farmyard, in the dark, John led us in a few vigorous physical exercises, gave us some simple instructions for the day, and then sent us off for tea before the first long sit began.

It was cold, I was sleepy, and I did not like having to sit still for hours on end. As the sessions of calming the mind proceeded I wondered why on earth I had come. My mind drifted off into fantasy, wild speculations, and thoughts of how long it was until the next meal; I felt my head jolting as I dropped into microsleeps, and full blown hallucinations attacked me. Then I jerked myself awake, angry with myself for drifting off. Great meditation! But I got through it.

The next day was quite different. I grabbed every chance I could to sleep, even for a few minutes, and began to feel better. In the muddy yard, in the early morning darkness, John gave us an odd instruction, to 'look and see what constrains your present experience'. I was surprised to find that some quite complicated things did not. For example, thoughts about the next break, why I'd bothered to come at all, or even sex, were easy to let go of once I'd noticed them. On the other hand some kinds of thought were definitely constraining my present experience: thoughts about myself, what other people thought of me, my plans to make up for some past misdemeanour, and imaginary conversations with people I wanted to impress. They went round and round, blah blah blah, on and on; even tunes running in my head. How silly. Yet observing them come and go, hour after hour, did seem to calm the mind. The torrent of confusion and self-criticism slowed just a touch.

It was later on this second day that John gave us the first of the questions. He read slowly from Tipun's notebook.

> To examine the basis of the mind abiding (in tranquillity) and the mind moving (with thought) it is necessary to look into the following questions:
>
> When abiding in tranquillity what is the nature of such abiding?
>
> What is the manner whereby it is maintained?
>
> How does the movement of thought arise within tranquillity?
>
> Is there an essential difference between abiding in tranquillity and moving in thought?

I had never done anything like this before. The questions were so strange. But I loved being given something concrete to do instead of the usual 'Make your minds bright, 30 minutes' of John's Zen instructions. So I set to work to observe the tranquillity and the moving in thought. The trouble was, there was a lot more of the latter than the former.

I persevered. Another hour-long session went by. And another. Now I began to notice gaps. Is this the tranquillity between the thoughts? Am I abiding in it? If so, what is the nature of such abiding?

It seemed to mean sitting in a world full of sights and sounds that changed, and came and went, while nothing really moved. The idea of moving in thought then made sense. The tranquillity itself seemed to be maintained by attention to the birds singing, or to the floor in front of me, or to the silence between.

A phrase came to mind from a famous Zen story in which a man asked the Zen master Ikkyu to write down some words of great wisdom. Ikkyu wrote 'attention'. Not satisfied, the man asked for more, so Ikkyu wrote 'attention, attention'. Still not satisfied, he demanded more, and Ikkyu wrote 'attention, attention, attention'.

This seemed, however, to be a rather special kind of attention; something like paying attention equally to everything without making any choices. As for the thoughts arising within tranquillity, that was a bit harder. They came all right but I could not see from where. So I sat and watched as thoughts came apparently out of nowhere, repetitive thoughts, thoughts set off by sounds around me, thoughts induced by people coughing or sneezing, irritating thoughts of the 'aren't I doing well?' kind followed by 'No I'm not. Oh stop it! Pay attention!' Still, for all my failures, this task made thoughts something to be observed rather than criticised, and I began to see thought as one aspect and abiding in tranquillity as another. So I had the answer! They are both the same.

Someone tapped me on the shoulder. My turn. My heart beat faster. I stood up, bowed to the cushion, and slipped out of the meditation hall.

A traditional part of many Buddhist retreats is an interview with the Master; either a formal interview following set rules, or an informal one more like a normal conversation. This was to be an informal interview. I climbed the creaky stairs to the bedroom at the back of the house, stooped under the faded Indian curtain hanging over the door, and found John sitting, dressed in his master's robes, facing an empty chair. I bowed, sat down in the empty chair, and blurted out how hard I'd been finding the retreat. He kindly suggested that my tales of tiredness and hallucination might contain a hint of self-pity, and suggested how to combat them. Then I told him my answer to the question.

'Yes', he said, 'That is the classic Mahamudra answer. Still, there is a difference. Do you know what it is?' I didn't. I said I'd try to think about what it was. 'Not now', he said, 'I just thought you might have noticed.' I felt deflated. But I went back to work determined to find out.

That night I drifted into sleep very alert. Something observed something else falling asleep. Something heard the boards clapped together at half past five in the morning, and seemed to be still awake, though quite refreshed. I was quickly up and out into the rain.

All that day I stared into the moving mind and the tranquil mind and had no idea what the difference was, except that one was still and one was moving. Ah. But what is moving? That might help. I thought it might be the self. Of course. Yes. It's the self that moves. I wanted to rush back to John and tell him proudly that I had an answer. But there were no interviews that day. I could put myself on the list for one the following day, but I felt embarrassed to be the first person to do so. So I set myself to exploring every change to see whether my hypothesis worked. And then somehow I got angry. I don't know why, or how, but I seemed to be angry at everyone and everything; at people who made too much noise, at the stupid chanting and visualisations that we had to do between the sessions of meditation, at the cold, at John sitting there so composed, at the lack of sleep, and at myself.

I was angry that I was angry, and angry that I couldn't get on with the task. Everything seemed foggy and unreal. I didn't want to be there. I didn't want to be like this.

Curiously, it was one of the Tibetan visualisations that dispelled the anger. We had to visualise an extremely complicated series of actions involving becoming a creature with four arms; the arms representing emptiness, love, countless beings and compassion.

I followed the instructions obediently, although I'd always thought these intricate Tibetan practices rather silly. Yet somehow this exercise undermined all the anger and swept it away. In Buddhism it is often stressed that compassion and insight must go together, and although I am writing here almost entirely about insight, this practice was one of many that showed me the importance of balance. It seems that anger can't survive much compassion.

At the end of this exercise I went to the outside toilet, at the back of the house. It has rough wooden walls that smell pungently of creosote, and a torn flowery curtain for a door. It was there, staring quietly at the creosoted wall and visualising countless suffering beings, that the anger just melted away. It was impossible to be angry with all those beings who were just the same as everything else. I couldn't be angry with that woman who kept sneezing all the time when the sneezing was just a noise. Oddly enough, seeing people as less like people and more like ghosts, made compassion easier, not harder.

This clarity was soon gone, and I was back to worrying about that interview, my answer to the question, and what John would say. I had finally put my name on the list and was impatient for the time to come. But now John gave us a new question from the notebook. We had to inquire into whether the awareness that observes the states of abiding and moving is the same or different from the states themselves. This, he said (perhaps by way of encouragement), was preparation for seeing everything as having 'one taste' and finally to step into 'non-meditation'.

What? The idea of everything having one taste seemed abhorrent – even though he described it as 'the refreshing taste of emptiness'. Differences and contrasts are what make life worth living. And what about non-meditation? If that's the goal then why are we spending all these years learning to meditate?

But I was meant to be asking about the observer. Am I the awareness that observes? Logic did no good. So I sat and watched.

And as I watched I began to feel respect for whoever had constructed this Mahamudra. When I went to bed I realised that I wasn't even fretting about whether I was doing well or doing badly. I was greedy for more meditation which was odd because I'd always looked on the keen meditators as quite a different species from myself. But I was deeply confused about this latest question and wanted to keep on working.

The next day dawned bright and clear. We took one of the meditation sessions outside, looking out over the wide valley with its interminable heather and bleating sheep. A deep calm came over me. The time for my interview came and I found myself saying I did not need it any more. Everything seemed the same now. I realised that it wouldn't have mattered whether John said I was right (in which case I'd have thought 'goody goody, clever me') or wrong (in which case I'd have thought 'Oh no, I'm a failure, stupid me'). His question had dissolved in the next question and was gone.

As I sat under a wind-stunted hawthorn tree, in my three shirts, two jumpers, two coats and a blanket, everything had the same taste and there was nothing to be done. The others were dotted around the hill. John was at the door of his room. The tiny cars moved silently far away down the valley, and the clouds drifted across the wide sky. When the bell rang I unwrapped my blanket and picked my way down the hill through the vivid rough grass, and back to the meditation hall.

I am back in my garden shed. It's fourteen years since that first Mahamudra retreat; ten years since I last spent a week all alone at the farmhouse in the Welsh hills, working my way yet again through Tipun's series of questions, reading just one or two each morning and then spending all day inquiring into them.

It's January. It's windy. It's wet.

I lay the tattered old photocopy from all those years ago carefully in front of my cushion and read the familiar words:

> Insight meditation is established through examining the root of (both) abiding and moving and then meditating within the experience of non-elaboration.
>
> To examine the basis of the mind abiding (in tranquillity) and the mind moving (with thought) it is necessary to look into the following questions:
>
> When abiding in tranquillity what is the nature of such abiding?
>
> What is the manner whereby it is maintained?
>
> How does the movement of thought arise within tranquillity?
>
> Is there an essential difference between abiding in tranquillity and moving in thought?

I begin with the first question. 'When abiding in tranquillity …'. Ha. It's all a trick. How many times have I thought that. The only point of these questions is to lure you into tranquillity. The answers don't matter. But maybe that's OK.

I sit. The wind blows. In a brief lull in the rain, the cat creeps in and sleeps for an hour next to me. It's too windy for birds.

It's the fourth day. I've been working hard these past three days, but today is not good. There was a terrible storm in the night. The banging and crashing woke me many times. I am tired and sleepy. I don't know how a fog can be made of thoughts but it is. There seems to be no gap between them, no space into which to peek even to look for tranquillity.

I sit with it. I don't get angry. I accept the irritation. Years ago I might have raged against my own mind, but now I know the fog will either clear or it will not. I want to work with the question but if I can't, I can't. I sit.

I take a break and run up and down the steps by the garage, a simple way of getting warm; ten times up and down, then round the apple trees and back to sitting again. Another session passes. I am outside again. This time I smash some wood for the fire and get hot with the exertion, damp leaves blowing past me in the fierce wind. I go back to the hut and slowly light some incense sticks.

It's clear. There it is. Tranquillity. Where did that come from?

Keep steady, and ask 'What is the nature of abiding?'

I sit for a while. It's something like this, I think. The attention is steady – or at least it leans only slightly from this to that. Something – the space around me, the ground before my eyes – stays steady. Leaves are scudding past my door, getting stuck on the small puddles and then freeing themselves and scudding on again; the fence behind is crashing with sudden force as it flips against a tree. But if I think of them that way then the bare attention is lost. Once they become leaves and fence, attention is all gathered up into objects and the tranquillity is gone. So I stop asking and keep practising. I see and hear and feel but name nothing.

So it goes on. Stuff happens.

And how is tranquillity maintained? By paying attention. But this is not the kind of focused attention that brings out details or applies concentration to one thing. In fact it is just the reverse. It is something like paying attention equally to everything.

There's a problem here. What is everything? As soon as I think about everything then I think about particular things; and then there's thingness and division, and the sense of attending to everything is lost in the attempt.

I take a few steadying breaths, and pay attention. It gets easier. Something stabilises.

Ready? Yes. How do thoughts arise within tranquillity?

This seems too easy. Here I am sitting peacefully, alert, paying attention. Everything is steady and in balance. It's easy and natural. Surely when a thought appears I will see it coming and I'll be able to answer the question.

I go on sitting. Stuff happens, paying attention.

Oops. What? To my astonishment I find I'm half way through a great long line of thought about how the bird table fell over in the wind and whether it would be better to pick it up now or leave it until the wind has died down in case … Someone had been having all those thoughts and I didn't notice! Who didn't notice? The one who was supposed to be asking the question? Who's she?

Oh dear. Stop and begin again. You know this happens. You know that thoughts do that. But I want to see where they come from, and how they arise in tranquillity. That train of thought was presumably provoked by the sound of a bird, or a gust of wind, but I was watching for it wasn't I? How could I have failed to notice all those thoughts for so long?

I'm reminded of the parallel threads. There was someone sitting in tranquillity, waiting for a thought to come along so that she could see how it arose, but she didn't see it. Meanwhile a great long complicated thought started up and suddenly the two collided. Oops. Did the one asking the question carry on while another one had started thinking? Or did the thought think itself, or … ?

I'm not supposed to be asking a thousand supplementary questions. Get back to work. How do thoughts arise in tranquillity?

The day wears on and tranquillity stabilises. A headless body sits calmly in the garden shed. Stuff happens.

I take another break and make a cup of tea. I keep a kettle in the shed, and a little jug of milk so I don't have to go back to the house. I pour the boiling water carefully, and hold the cup gently, still paying attention to the floor, the wind and the sounds of rain now beating on the roof.

I sit down again, slowly, and pay attention. I ask 'Is there an essential difference between the mind abiding in tranquillity and the mind moving in thought?' I should be able to ask this question now that the mind is indeed abiding tranquilly. I wonder whether I should make thoughts deliberately and look to see whether they are different. I don't see why I shouldn't. I'm allowed to if I want.

I sit still a bit longer and then start deliberately thinking. It's maddeningly difficult to do this after spending so long watching for thoughts to arise as though they were the enemy. I pick on a theme, set it going and then try to watch. The odd thing is that when I do this I'm still paying open attention, and so nothing seems to move. I wonder how to let the mind move and examine its moving without holding it back. I seed some thoughts and let them loose, and watch, and hope to catch them out again after they've gone, and round and round. It reminds me of William James trying to catch hold of the flights between the perchings in the 'bird's life' of the mind. At least I have something to do.

In experimenting this way I find there are two different kinds of thought. First there are those that happen right here, in the midst of tranquillity, like asking the question and watching for an answer. These thoughts feel part of the space in which I'm sitting. They don't distract the mind, and the mind doesn't seem to move. At least, it moves only in the way that the branches of that distant tree are moving, or the ripples of wind on the puddle are moving. They move and don't move.

Then there are those protracted streams of complicated thoughts that seem to catch me out. They move all right. But it's more than that. It's as though they start without me. They drag part of the mind away and then, since I'm so bad at catching them out, the mind seems split in two before I even notice.

In a flash of thought that seems to take no time at all I can see all this laid out as a theory about what is happening in the brain, with groups of neurons organising themselves in different places, their patterns arising and falling away, though with no need of an experiencing self. But if I try to put it into words it seems fiercely complicated and the attempt is distracting. It doesn't matter. I won't forget the vivid wordless mental image summoned up. I can think about it later.

I go back to watching the moving mind and the mind abiding in tranquillity.

It's my last break of today. So I take up the notes and read the same page over again. I read the now familiar questions slowly, letting the words well up within tranquillity. I come to the next line, which I have not read so far this week:

> It then becomes important to examine whether the awareness that does the looking into these matters is separate from the abiding and moving states or whether it is the same.
>
> There are three ways of investigating the experience of non-elaboration. This is done through inquiring into the reality of contrasts between (i) the three times of past, present and future, (ii) ...

I laugh. No. It's too much. I haven't even begun to think about time. How amazing this notebook is. That's enough for today.

I settle down again on my stool and abide in tranquillity.

Or do I? There's always some little movement isn't there? Now slightly towards the bird song, just started up as the wind begins to ease; now slightly towards the gloss of rain on the flagstones in front my eyes; now just a tiny shift towards the feel of the cushion beneath me. What if my mind does not move at all? What if attention is completely steady, completely without elaboration? Is there anything at all left when nothing is leant towards, nothing away from. I look. It's ...

6

There is no time. What is memory?

A week with a koan

One January, John Crook ran a new kind of retreat at Maenllwyd. The idea was for people to spend a whole week working on just one koan. It sounded ideal for me. So I signed up, arriving in the mountains along with twenty or so others, on a bitterly cold winter's evening.

The first day, after the usual early rising and morning's meditation, John read out a list of a dozen or so koans. Some were traditional Zen stories, one was a story of his own, and others were short questions. I liked some of the stories, and was reminded of them in the days to come, but one short koan stood out: 'There is no time. What is memory?' It was an inscription John had seen on the arch of a Chinese temple on Lantau Island in Hong Kong. When he'd finished reading the list, he handed us copies with a list of instructions, and sent us off for a short walk, to read quietly by ourselves and choose one to be our companion for a whole week. I climbed the steep track on the other side of the stream and sat on a flat promontory looking out over the valley. As instructed, I studied them all carefully in case my decision had been too hasty, but no. This one was obviously for me.

The routine of the retreat got under way. We rose each day at 5 a.m. for energetic exercises in the frozen yard followed by a few words of encouragement and advice; then a quick cup of tea before the first meditation session of the day. Apart from meals, work periods and a walk in the afternoon, the routine was mostly half-hour meditation sessions broken by ten-minute breaks for slow walking in the yard, or exercises indoors. Our task was clear: to keep our chosen koan firmly in mind all the time and never let it go.

The first morning, when we'd all assembled under the bright stars of a frosty morning in the yard and dutifully copied John's assorted jumps and stretches, he gave us some steadying words for the day: 'Patience, Application, Persistence'.

I start work. The instruction sheet says that Western minds will first tackle the koan intellectually, but that this thinking will naturally wear itself out, so not to worry. Good. I don't have to prevent myself from thinking, or feel guilty about it. If thinking wears itself out that's fine. Until then, I'll think.

My first approach is to lay out the territory. What I have is simple: here a statement; there a question. I don't need to rush. I have a whole week to tackle this koan. I decide to take the statement and sit with it in two different ways. First I'll agree with it, and then later I'll disagree with it. So, first, I will agree that there is no time.

I sit. I look. I look very hard. I sit and look at the carpet on the floor in front of me. But I haven't had enough sleep. That's the one thing I hate about these organised retreats. I don't get enough sleep and so I cannot concentrate properly. I start to hallucinate.

The pattern of colours and squiggles on the carpet turns into big crabs that get up and crawl about over each other and make me blink and get cross. But I cannot see any time. OK then. The koan is right. There is no time. But if there is no time, what is memory?

I am out in the yard again, for slow walking meditation, looking down at the ground as I pace up and down. The frost has gone, and the mud and sheep droppings squelch under my feet. The sky is heavy with scudding clouds. Of course there's time. The clouds are pouring up straight into the sky from behind the hills, moving fast. You can't have movement without time. The movement of the clouds only makes sense in time. The koan is wrong. There is time.

Hours of sitting pass. The crabs crawl and I blink to keep myself awake.

Hang on a minute. How can I tell the clouds have moved, or hear that noise as a cough, or see that John is walking? Because from one moment to the next I can *remember* what came before. Without memory they would be meaningless sights and sounds. And what is memory? Ha. This is a clever koan indeed. If I agree with it, then I become perplexed about memory – for how can you have memory without time? But if I disagree with it I have to find out what time is. I begin to feel a curious respect for these seven simple words.

It's evening and we all sit in deep silence around a flickering log fire, the smell of the smoke hanging heavy in the slowly warming house. I stare at the flames. They are moving all the time. Their very nature is movement: they couldn't be flames if they stayed still. So is there time in these flames? Is there a now? I could grasp a moment with a camera but there is no camera, only my eyes, and what they see keeps on changing. I can't grasp a moment from which to say that what has gone before is past and what is to come next is future.

I watch the tongues of red curling around the dried bark of a long-dead tree and try to imagine things from the flames' point of view. Flames have no memory, so can they have time? Staring hard into the flickering lights I can see that from their point of view there is no time: they cannot have a past, a now and a present. I get the creepiest feeling that the whole of the universe is like this. Flames, and pieces of wood, and rocks, and fireplaces, and matches, and hills – none of them has time. I sit and listen to the crackling.

An ant is crawling from the pile of wood on the floor. Is there time from an ant's point of view? The ant is different from stones and hills. I wonder whether this is what it means to be a sentient being, but I don't know. There is so much to investigate. A week seems nothing. But it's late. I wash, clean my teeth, and slip into my sleeping bag, still holding my koan steadily in mind.

This is how far I got with my koan the first day.

The morning boards are sounding and I'm instantly awake. The words are right here. 'There is no time. What is memory?'

On this second day the complicated thoughts keep coming, but not so fast. I'm slowing down and becoming more mindful. My respect for this koan, or for whoever invented it, is growing. It is like a magic converter that flips everything in its path into mindfulness; and it does so without a jerk, or discontinuity; just a little switch. For example, I might begin meandering off into thoughts like, 'I remember when I was here last summer when the ...', but before I can get lost in reminiscence up come the words, 'What is memory?' So instead of being cross with myself for the lapse in concentration, and tugging myself back to the present with a jolt, the memory itself becomes food for the koan 'What is this memory?' I can watch those images of last summer and ask; what is this? The same is true of almost every thought that comes up in meditation. I begin to see that most are memories, or built on memories, in one form or another. So through every arising thought I am still working on the koan. Or perhaps the koan is working on me.

This morning, in the yard, where we all stood shivering or gazing dumbstruck at the beauty of night in the mountains, John gave his advice for the day: 'Perfect practice' (ha!), 'Persistence' (again), and 'Let the koan do it.' It seems that it is; the koan is doing something.

It is the third day and we are each to have a formal interview with John in the library, a small wooden room with books and a narrow bed, tacked onto the end of the barn. We have been told to enter quietly, bow to a particular statue, sit down on the cushion facing John, and then, without him having to ask or say anything, explain how far we have got with our koan.

I have heard so many Zen stories of encounters between teachers and monks. They are always dramatic or insightful, and either teacher or pupil does something unexpected. At the end the monk is either chastised and told to keep practising, or instantly

becomes enlightened. Of course I want to become enlightened –
to be hit with a stick and everything falls away and then … stop it.
I want John to approve of me, to think I'm clever, that I'm getting
on really well with my koan. I know all this from many retreats. It's
just self-centred stuff that gets in the way. I know. I concentrate
hard, waiting for my turn. There's a tap on my shoulder. I get up,
bow and walk slowly and mindfully to the library.

I push the curtain door aside, find the right statue and bow to
it, sit on the empty cushion, pause, and then bang twice on the
floor.

'What separates these two bangs?' I ask, as John sits perfectly
still in front of me. 'Time of course. So the koan is wrong. There
is time. But we only see the time when we remember one bang
from the other. And what is memory? This is a very clever koan.
From here you can begin to doubt all past things, and all future
things too, because they are all built on memory. So all that's left is
now. You can't doubt that – can you? But what is it? I am looking
to see. That's how far I have got with my koan.'

I feel pleased with myself. I said it clearly and well.

John is impassive. 'Fine', he says.

'Aren't you going to help me?' I ask.

He smiles and says 'Continue.'

I walk back to my place in the hall, and continue.

I'm going to try another tack. If I can't catch a 'now' perhaps I can
find what's happening now; one might say 'the *contents* of now'.
This might be easier because I can look into whatever it is that I

am seeing, or hearing, or feeling, or remembering, at that moment. I realise that this is the same concept as 'the contents of consciousness' so familiar in neuroscience. Yes, this is my consciousness; it's my 'now'. I shall look into that.

I stare at the carpet crabs, and the unstable streaks of the wooden floor. I open my ears to the cracking of logs in the stove, to the shuffling of other people's uncomfortable knees, and to the clearing of throats of my fellow koan-strugglers. I try to feel how it feels to have a slight pain in my calves. The more I look the less substantial the feelings seem. The longer I watch, the less like sounds and sights and feelings they are. Yet these are all the contents of 'now'. What is this? What is this?

I am surprised to realise that this is the very same question that drives my life; that motivates my research, and has done for decades: 'What is consciousness?' This is all I want to do: to sit, quiet and steady, and ask this question. Surely I must be able to see if I look hard enough, mustn't I? I must keep looking, all the time, meditating or not meditating.

It's work period now, and I have been assigned to care for the twin-vault, urine-separating, composting toilets. I love them. I like the principle of dealing with waste without water, and the skilful job of tending them properly. I like working on my own in mindful silence, and getting the bathrooms sparkly clean. I have got the smell under control, and they are working perfectly. But the people drive me mad. They come and want to use the toilets during work time (why aren't they doing their own jobs?), or even to speak to me (don't they know what silence means?). But I persevere. I don't look at people on retreats – not at all. I look at feet. It is a long habit stemming from something that Master Sheng Yen said many years ago. 'Make no eye contact, make no facial expression, just bow in acknowledgement and gratitude to others.' So I let the others be ghosts in shoes, and I mop the floor. Is this now?

This is a magic koan. It gobbles up everything in its path. Even repeating the words 'There is no time' requires memory. It is a self-gobbling koan. I am looking to see what is left after everything is gobbled up.

Sounds, tastes, the carpet in front of my eyes; what are they like? Whether I try looking for the 'now', or ask what is *in* the 'now', I stumble into a kind of blindness, a fog, an inability to see what I'm looking right at. It's as though out of the corner of my eye I'm convinced that something's there, but when I look straight at it I cannot see. Things somehow evaporate into insubstantiality whenever I am looking at them.

In one way this blindness is encouraging. On a retreat many years ago, I remember Sheng Yen telling us that we had to become blind and deaf, and I had no idea what he meant. Indeed, I hated the idea because I desperately wanted to see more clearly – not the reverse. But if he advocates blindness, then maybe I'm getting somewhere.

But it's horrible. I hate it! I'm getting angry. I keep staring into the blindness harder and harder. I don't know how to proceed. Keep looking – can't see. Keep looking – it runs away. Keep listening – can't hear. Look. Look. Pay attention!

I remember that the koan is meant to be doing it, not me, and I relax a little. This helps. It even seems that *I am* the koan as I walk through the refectory and sit at my place at table. I am the koan as food is silently eaten. I am the koan as legs walk back across the yard. In some way that I don't understand this seems to open up a little chink. The wretched carpet glows spaciously.

Something has changed. Ha, this is interesting. (I allow myself a little academic speculation.) It's something like this. Normally, as my attention shifts here and there, there is a jump. First, some sounds or sights or pains seem to be right there, in my consciousness, and then I switch my attention and others come into consciousness. It is as though there is a me watching, and a space called 'my conscious mind' into which things come and go. I know this doesn't correspond to anything inside the brain. It would imply a kind of Cartesian Theatre: an impossible inner space where a ghost in the machine observes its stream of private experiences, with all the philosophical absurdities that that entails. Yet it has always seemed to be that way.

Now it doesn't seem like that at all. It seems as though everything I attend to was already happening. There's no jump or sudden discontinuity when my attention shifts. Everything is just as it is, or always was, even as it changes. I reflect that maybe experiences simply don't exist in ordered time. There is no 'now' of an experience itself, or a time at which 'I' experience it, or it 'comes into' my consciousness. Unlike the usual view, this could fit with how brains work, because all brain processes take time to unfold, and there is no special place or process in the brain which converts them into conscious experiences. There is no 'pontifical neuron', as William James would have put it; no 'central headquarters', as Dan Dennett would say. And if there isn't, then it is impossible to say what I am conscious of now, because there's no such thing. There are multiple brain processes going on, some of which take up more of the brain's capacity than others, but there is no me who experiences them, and no time at which they become conscious. How slow I am, but now I see that directly.

Thank goodness for the afternoon walks. The hill behind the house is steep and I'm breathing hard by the time I reach the edge of the moor with its heath, and sheep, and far views of the Welsh mountains. I plod along narrow sheep tracks, through the rough stalks of heather, walking steadily, staying mindful, asking my question as I go. The heather and rocks pass through me as I walk. I don't know who is walking, and I don't know who's moving, them or me.

Then I'm laughing and laughing and laughing. There are no 'contents of consciousness'! Of course. It's so obvious. Experiences are scraps; they're not grounded; they are not *in* anything; they're not centred anywhere, either in time or space. The world we think we see or hear – is always a memory. And what is memory? Ha ha!

I am grateful to this amazing koan; to this transforming, self-gobbling meme, to these circumstances here in mid-Wales, to my parents and to this little sturdy, willing body for which I suddenly feel much affection. My downfall is yet to come.

It's the second to last day and I am throwing myself even more fiercely into looking for the 'now'. The 'blindness' is intense, but it isn't anything as tangible as blindness, making it all the more frustrating. I can't find the 'now'; I can't see what anything is like, even though it's right in front of me. So I feel as though I can't see at all.

Why don't I just stop trying? I stop trying and fall into spaciousness and deep quiet. But I don't rest there; I want to understand; I want to keep *looking*.

Standing in the yard, staring blindly out over the beautiful scenery, I get the most powerful impression that if someone taps me on the shoulder I will explode. I'm quivering, on the edge of something terrifying.

No one does.

Sheep go on bleating.

It's my last interview and I'm so frustrated that I just shout at John, really loud. I want him to understand. He's sitting calmly in his robes, and I'm frothing and screaming inside.

'You talk glibly', I accuse him, 'about the answer to "what is this?" being "just this", but there is no "this", is there? I can't see a "this". Can you?'

He doesn't tell me whether he can or not, and I want to know.

'I can see you', he calmly replies.

I'm shouting back, 'That's not good enough' (because obviously in my frame of mind there could be no such simple thing as seeing someone).

'What's this all about?' he asks, and I explain about Sheng Yen and the blindness, and there being no now, and no contents of now.

'Ah yes', he says. 'You've entered the Great Doubt.'

That great Zen phrase sums it up to perfection. It's not just an intellectual, wordy doubt, but a doubt about every aspect of every experience. What is this? This? and This? I have no idea any more. I want him to tell me – to tell me how to look differently; how to see through to the world in a different way. He would not, or could not. Perhaps it is not like that. As I leave he tells me to take it a little more slowly.

A little more slowly!! When I'm bursting with … well, with what? There's nothing to do but follow his advice. I feel deflated. The passion and tension leak away. I go back to my place with tears drying on my face and get on with sitting.

My knees hurt. For the first time on this retreat, I feel pain in my knees. The meditation is more like it usually is on retreat: tedious, an effort, boring. I plod on.

'Stuff that' I think, after a welcome tea break. I'm not a Buddhist. I haven't taken any vows. I'm not devoted to doing whatever real Buddhists would do in this situation. I want to find out about the mind, and this great effort of inquiry seems to work, so I'm going to do it again, whatever he says.

I start on a new tack. Do past and future look different? I call up examples of each and look at them one by one. For the past I remember years ago, when I lived in Pear Tree Cottage and the children were small. I see them playing in the garden. I can visualise the layout and see them running about. It has a certain feel to it: mind feel, imagination. OK, so now for some future. I think about when I'm going to leave Maenllwyd at the end of the week.

I imagine getting in my car and turning carefully in the muddy yard. I imagine driving down the valley, opening and closing all those gates for the sheep. I can visualise the layout and see the twists and turns of the track. It has a certain feel to it: mind feel.

They're all just the same stuff – memory stuff; imagination stuff. Past and future can be held in mind as equivalent. What then comes between them? The 'now' is supposed to, of course, yet I have already realised that it cannot be found. There is no longer a past, a present and a future, laid out in a line with me moving along in the middle. It simply isn't like that any more. The question 'What is memory?' turns out to be the same question as 'What is this?'

So what is all this stuff? How, and where, and when, is it arising?

It's the last day of the retreat and I set to work again, looking into the whatever it is. I conjure up past things, and future things, and completely imaginary things, and present things. Although I can label them differently, and they vary in vividness and how much confidence I have in their details, they all seem to be made of the same kind of stuff. It is somehow manifesting itself, but how? And where? And when? As I say goodbye to John I tell him that I have a new question, 'When is this experience?' He laughs. We laugh together and I feel close to him as I leave.

Before driving away I walk up on to the rainy, windy hill, where everything is movement and change. I'm being mindful, but then I have a sudden thought. After so many years of practice, there is one thing I thought I could rely on; that I know what mindfulness is. It is being fully here in the present moment. But now I know that there is no such moment. So what is mindfulness? I know it's different from not being mindful. But how?

So this is what I am left with at the end of this retreat. The one thing I really thought I had learned in all these years is overthrown.

7

When are you?

It's spring time. At least, at home the crocuses and daffodils are already in flower, but spring has yet to arrive at Maenllwyd. The hillside looks bleak as I drive into the muddy yard and drag my case and sleeping bag into the house, to find my designated bed space and see what job I've been allocated for the week.

The others are arriving. I don't like to talk but John insists that we all sit round the fire and introduce ourselves before we go into silence. He tells us that the first thing is to arrive; to be here in the presence of the given, here and now. Over all these years this place has seeped into me. It feels as though it and I are part of the same arriving. I'm not separate from this old house, the muddy yard, and the two great sycamore trees that I know so well. It's odd to realise how much of oneself is not inside, but out there. I think of old people with failing memories who need their familiar places. Part of who they are remains in the walls, and tables, and steps that they see every day. So part of me is this house and this yard.

I lay out my bed, my extra rugs, my few simple warm clothes, and get firmly back into the habit of not looking at anyone, and being mindful. Tonight a short sit and bed. Tomorrow the koan.

Day one, and my koan for the week is already proving more varied and interesting than it appeared at first sight. I chose it, sitting on a rock half way up the track, where there's a view right down the valley. The words leapt out at me when John read his list. I was worried that it was too close to my previous koan 'There is no time. What is memory?', and I might get bored, or learn nothing new. But leap it did, and I chose it. So here I sit, the first day, ready to begin asking 'When are you?'

It's obviously about time and self, I think, but I'll just feel my way around the question before I work out what to do next. Thoughts shift around. I'm still settling in. I'm trying to be mindful. And, ah. This question promotes mindfulness of itself. As I'm sitting here, and thoughts come up that drag me away from the mindful present, they are mostly of the 'I wonder if …', or 'I remember when …', 'I wish …' variety. In their self-centredness, they remind me of the question 'When are you?' and I'm propelled back both to the present and to the question. So far so good. I can work with this.

There are three words. So how about tackling each in turn? (I faintly wonder whether I can really spend an entire week doing nothing but thinking about three words – and three very ordinary words at that!) But I'm being mindful. Don't think about a whole week, it'll only terrify you. Be here, now, and concentrate.

When? The whole of the first day I sit and watch the thoughts prompted by that simple first word: When? Memories arise. That holiday was years ago. Yes, but when? I realise I'm constructing a series of years and dates, and placing that holiday in position along it. I'm remembering what the builder said last Thursday, and visualising my diary with its whole structure of days and weeks, and the order in which things happen. Really the thought is happening now, isn't it?

I see myself at home in the kitchen. When was that? Do I mean when did the event I am remembering actually happen? Surely not, because I cannot remember it precisely. Indeed it's probably an amalgam of many such times when I've stood in the same kitchen, doing similar tasks. So it's impossible to say when it was by objective time. So I must mean when is the memory happening? I would say that it's happening now, except that now's already slid past.

I start looking for the now in which I am remembering these past events, but each of these thoughts takes some time to unfold and there is no 'now' within them to be grasped. They come, they take their time and they go. Neither the beginning, nor the end, nor the middle means much without the rest. It seems that neither the time at which the original event occurred, nor the time at which I am remembering it can be pinned down.

'When' is very confusing. I must just keep at it.

We sit. We walk in the yard. We carry out our jobs in silence, and eat our meals in the dusty refectory at the side of the house. I'm kitchen assistant. I carry the dishes mindfully, not looking up, placing them in front of people whose eyes I never meet. When?

It's the second day. I'm settling into the place, into mindfulness, into really being here. The weather is fabulous: cold, frosty mornings when we're up in the dark and out in the yard; clear, cold days with the palest blue sky and a watery sun. There are new spring lambs with high-pitched bleats, and old mountain ewes with deep, throaty 'baa's echoing interminably back and forth; the sonic background to all our meditations.

I'm on my cushion. I'm going to move on. I'm going to tackle 'are'. **Are**.

I feel 'you', or self, threatening to intrude, but I will stick to 'are'.

This seems a bit daft. What can I do with 'are'? Are; am; to be. To be or not to be … Stop it!

Of course, there's a simpler meaning to this question, something like 'When *are* you?' as opposed to 'When are you *not*?': something like 'When do you exist?' as opposed to 'When do you not exist?' This is about being here and not being here; about being mindful and not being mindful; about when these different states happen. I can work with this too.

Right now I am mindful. I am sitting here and concentrating. When is this? I try to flip back and forth between being here and not being here, but I can't. Whenever I am working on this koan I seem to be present. There is someone here doing the asking and it *is*. This is a familiar one, I realise. It's just like asking whether I'm conscious now. Whenever I ask the question the answer seems to be yes. Whenever I am asking, I am. I stare into it for a while. And another long time.

As the slow minutes tick by I get distracted into wondering when the bell will sound, how many more sessions it is before dinner, and thinking about a friend I should have rung last week. They are all self-related thoughts. So 'I' was in them. Thinking about almost anything brings up a 'me'. But I can see it's all fiction. It's all just thoughts whirling around an idea of me. Not yet. I'm not supposed to work on 'you' yet. I'm still on 'are'.

I start on a new tack. If I'm asking when I am and when I am not, then I'd better be able to look into both of them and ask when they begin and end, when they happen. But I can't. Every time I try to see when I am not, I fail. I can't see myself not being. Hmm.

OK. Let me try again. Can I somehow let go of myself and leap off into nothingness, so that I can know I wasn't then, and then come back and know that I am again? It sounds worth trying. All I have to do is to cease being. I must throw myself into non-being. I must let go.

Something flickers. For a moment I seem not to be; not to be anything at all, gone. But in a flash I'm back, asking the question. Did I really disappear? When was that? I laugh. I don't know.

OK, try again, let go, reappear, and then ask when. I get this slippery sense that if only I had the courage, or the skill, or something … then I'd be able to drop out of existence entirely and come back again, but it does not happen. Perhaps I am afraid that the me who comes back will not be the same one who disappeared. Indeed I know it will not.

There's something very peculiar about this. I begin to sense that I and the koan are inextricably linked. But I don't understand the feeling. I keep working. Are.

We are all to have interviews, and this time they are not with John but with one of his trainee teachers called Jake, with John sitting by. I await my turn. The tap on the shoulder comes. I walk mindfully into the library and sit down with the two of them.

Jake's eyes strike me in some way; alert, aware. Then out it all comes. I burble on about what I've been doing, and throw in the odd joke at John's expense, and we all laugh.

'Do you have any questions?' Jake asks.

I don't. I feel rather stupid for not having any questions. I say 'No' and just sit there.

'What is it like having no questions?' he says, and I'm stumped.

He repeats the question.

'It's just getting on with it.' I reply, and am dismissed.

I'm all shaken up as I sit back on my cushion. I can think of so many much better things I should have said, and I can't shake off thinking about them; such a pointless and stupid activity: wishing I'd done something different. I could have said, 'Nothing. There's nothing it's ever like to be anything.' That seems to be the conclusion I'm coming to, but I wonder whether I really mean it. Since the science of consciousness is all about 'What it's like to be' something, then this claim would be rather serious! It makes me laugh. I wonder whether Jake realised how pertinent his question was.

I could have said, 'Dead.'

I could have asked him all the questions I really want answers to, like, 'What is it that you know, and I don't?' or even 'When are you?'

It's pathetic. Stop it! I take a deep breath and get to work again. Are.

It's day three. Somewhere out there in the rest of the world it's Sunday. Forget that. Come on now. See the wooden floor and the carpet, hear the sheep and the crackling of the wood stove, pay attention! Today you are going to take up the third word, 'you'. **You**.

I can already see that there are several branches to this one. I begin to explore. I'm going to ask who I am, look at myself, and then throw in the 'when?'

This is fun. I have licence to think about myself. I remember when I was a little kid, with a big bandage on my arm from the operations I had on my hand. I see my parents' house with its garden and garage and path. I imagine myself at home … but stop. When is all this? It's both then and now, but I can't pin either down. These are fictions. Horrible fictions. They aren't real. They are just thoughts about a person bubbling up now, but what about now. Oh no. I can't bear that one again. I'm not going hunting for a now that I know I won't find. So when are you?

I start with myself again. I'm holding in mind a feeling of myself; a feeling that I know who I am; I am used to myself. I can throw up all these images but none of them is essential to who I am. The essential bit is this sense of familiarity in the midst of it all, which is me. William James referred to the 'warmth and intimacy' that marks a thought as being 'mine'. This warmth and intimacy and immediacy, he said, give rise to the continuity of certain chosen portions of the past, to the community of self, and to the connections between memories that make them 'mine'. But I know as soon as the thought begins to roll out that I'm kidding myself. This too is just another feeling, right here, bubbling up and falling away again. And when is that?

There is someone asking the question, isn't there?

This morning, after exercises in the yard, John said that everyone will tackle their koan in their own way; as gloomy or fun, as science or philosophy, as poetry or pain; but whichever it is we must not forget to move on.

'Hold your koan' he said. This isn't difficult. I am working hard and the koan does not leave me, at least not for long. I'm encouraged as we file into the hall to sit.

Every day we get up in the cold dark and the sun slowly rises during that first hour's meditation. Today we emerge from the meditation hall into a brilliant world of bright sun gleaming off a dense white hoarfrost that falls away down the mountainside into a rippling valley fog. Tears well up. I stare. When is this?

In his daily lecture John talks about the 'mirror mind'. I have heard the phrase before but I don't know what it is. He says that in the Chan practice of 'Silent Illumination' you have to open the mirror mind, and not do anything with it. But here our task is to prepare the mirror mind and then drop the koan into it. Hmm. I've no idea what he's talking about.

But I've plenty to do. If there's someone asking the question then I can ask when that person is, can't I?

This is fun too. Sit down, ask the question; look into who's asking and then ask, 'When is this?' I was unprepared. I was caught unawares.

'When are you?' I'm the questioner asking the question. I turn back to ask the questioner 'When are you?' and it's the question asking me who's asking the question and …

It's all gone wrong. The question is hovering right there in front of my face but I'm not sure whether I'm the question or the face. But anyway it's not the face at all, it's whatever lies behind the face. The question is staring into the space behind my face and is finding nothing but the question. It seems as though all my life there's been a skin or a veil between the me inside here and the world I can see out there – not a real skin, obviously. Indeed I've no idea what I mean, but now it's not there and I can sense something missing. The whole of my head is opened up. In fact there isn't any head at all, or back to it. It's as though I was looking in a mirror before, and now I'm not. There is no division. There is no back or front. No behind the mirror or in front of it, no inside or outside. The question is asking itself through me and I am …

I don't know, but I'm skilled enough to see that this is an opportunity, and I could blow it. Don't panic. You know what to do now. Remember the old Mahamudra teaching: to recognise and experience insight, and remain in the experience of non-elaboration. I don't elaborate. The question keeps asking itself. The glass isn't there. Everything is adrift but there's something gloriously refreshing about it. John's 'refreshing taste of emptiness'?

I'm scared. The work goes on and sustains me, but if I reflect on it, as occasionally I do, in spite of the mindfulness, I can see that everything is falling apart. I looked into myself and found only fictions. I looked into the questioner and found only the question. I've lost what sometimes seems like a safety barrier between me and the things that are going on, so they're right here, vivid and immediate but anchorless and unconnected. What is this?

The koan isn't finished with me, and I am still working through those branches of the final word 'you'. Then I realise that, with the glass gone, the question is not about me at all. Or if it is, it is equally about anything and everything else. Anything at all that comes up: thought, sound, action; anything – I can present it with the question, 'When are you?'

Tonight we have an unexpected treat. It's full moon and John replaces one of the evening meditation sessions with a walk down through the fields in the dark. We follow in single file, with the crisp moon shadows falling on the wet grass, the frost beginning to form, and our breaths steaming up into the air. Mindful. Go to bed mindful. But I don't know what mindfulness is. Never mind. You know what to do. Pay attention. Go to sleep paying attention.

It's the last day and I'm back on my cushion; same floor, same fire, same bleating of the sheep – or are they different sheep? Different bleats? No matter. To any of them I am going to say 'When are you?'

I begin. A bird shrieks out; a curlew I think. When are you? It's obvious, and loud. The great sound was suddenly there; it lasted for a while (or I could later remember it as having lasted for a while); and then it was gone. I can perceive its temporal form, its sonic shape, but when was it?

The fire is still crackling, as it does. When is that? I notice it's one of those backwards threads again; the crackling's been going on for some time but this me wasn't listening to it; I was busy with the curlew sound. Do I ask 'When are you?' of that unlistened-to crackling as well? I reason that I am supposed to be asking the experiences themselves when they are, so if I wasn't experiencing it at the time then it doesn't count. So it began only when I noticed it. Yes, but when I noticed it I could already remember it having been going on, as though I, or someone, had been listening for a while. In that case I must ask when it was; but it was already a memory by the time I noticed it.

Stop it! Stop it! It's all right to think but this is getting you nowhere. Look! Listen! Watch! And I do. And I see.

Each sound, or taste, or feel, or thought, has its own shape or form, its own way of being, but I can't find any beginnings or endings. Just so long as I'm hearing or seeing it, then it is what it is; with this form in time and space. But they aren't in time and space. I suppose I had assumed a framework of time and space in which each of them occurs, but it simply isn't like that as I watch and listen. It's as though the notions of time and space arise within the things themselves and disappear when they disappear. It's as though things persist only when I am conjuring them up – listening or watching for them – and when they stop existing I cannot say when or where they were.

This reminds me of the sensorimotor theory; of the idea that seeing is a kind of doing; that we get an illusion of seeing the whole world at once because we can always look again and conjure up the next bit just in time.

There is no more mirror; no distinction between self and the world. There is just this stuff springing up out of no-place and no-time, with no continuous someone to whom it appears. So what is this stuff and where is it coming from? I peer into the nothingness out of which it all seems to be manifesting itself. I can't imagine what it is. Physics, chemistry, neuroscience, psychology: they are not helping. This isn't like that. These things are just coming out of nothing and going back into nothing. But is it nothing? What are they made of? What's going on? Everything is like this. Everything, and I have no idea where it comes from – even right here in my own mindful experience.

I look harder, as though straining to see into the cracks between things will help. But as soon as I look I'm creating something, and it's the uncreated I'm trying to look into. I conceive the notion that it's time to leap into the source and disappear.

I'm scared. I'm scared. I'm scared.

The koan is still there. And I realise with some relief that it's probably not going away. If everything else falls apart the question will just go on asking itself. If I fall apart, the koan will still be there. I'm ready. I feel as though I'm on the edge of a cliff and ready to throw myself off. Or it's tinier than that. It's more like the top of a flagpole, or a wobbly stick that I'm stupidly clinging to the top of. Go on. Jump. Jump. Let go. You know you're just a fiction. There's nothing to lose. Go on.

But I cannot, or do not, or the whole idea was misguided. I am left, again, quivering at the edge, things happening in no place and no time, emerging out of nothing or something.

I'm tired.

8

Are you here now?

For the first time in my life I decide to put aside two whole weeks for meditation practice. I know lots of Buddhists do seven-week retreats, or even seven-year retreats. I admire them for their commitment and sometimes wonder whether I could ever do the same, but for now, for me, two weeks seems a lot.

Tipun's questions still intrigue me, and John's schedule includes another Mahamudra week, in December 2003. So, although I much prefer the simplicity and starkness of Zen or Chan retreats, I decide to go. I particularly want to have another go at Tipun's question 'What is the difference between the mind resting in tranquillity and the mind moving in thought?', and I think it should be easier with the help and support of a formal retreat. I'll spend a week on my own in my hut, and then go straight off to Wales. Meditating for a whole week before the retreat should surely help.

The week at home is tough, and cold, but good practice. I set off on the three-hour drive with plenty of enthusiasm, and arriving in the old familiar yard is a joy. Maenllwyd seems to welcome me into easy mindfulness, and I'm looking forward to the week. I must have forgotten what to expect.

The first day's sitting is a horrible shock. I find the meditation tough and the routine irksome. Instead of the long series of half-hour sits, with ten-minute breaks, that I'm used to, there are hour-long sitting periods with either only slight pauses, or completely different activities in between, such as chanting, visualisations and other Tibetan rituals. There are no bright walks around the yard; no exercises in the Chan hall to loosen up the limbs, and no slow deepening of the practice. On the one hand a full hour is too long for me to maintain concentration, and on the other the breaks are too full of activity and people. As usual, there are some people who don't get into a deep silence, and even some who start chatting in the breaks. So by the time the next hour comes along I'm distracted. By the end of the first day I reflect that I'm doing far less meditation than I did last week, but finding it much harder.

I want to go home.

To make it worse, I'm kitchen assistant again. I *hate* being kitchen assistant; chopping the vegetables and serving the food. You have to listen to instructions for the day's food; you have to work with others who seem to want to chat over the chopping. It's so hard to be mindful. The only bit I like is the washing up, alone with the water and the gradually cleaning pans. I like outdoor jobs, clearing sheep droppings from the yard, pulling up stinging nettles behind the barn, or almost anything that gets me out doing physical work in the fresh air, away from the others. But we are not supposed to *like* our jobs. They are an opportunity to practise mindfulness in all circumstances; to accept all tasks with equanimity.

I hate being kitchen assistant.

Even worse is the lack of sleep. These days I no longer get the terrifying or revolting hallucinations that used to plague me many years ago – the scenes of rape, or cruelty, or torture, or decay that used to beset my sleepy mind; but I still slide off into sleep, with my eyes unable to rest quietly on the floor. This sleep deprivation seems pointless. It is as though there is a window of opportunity between sleep and over-excitement into which clear meditation falls. All last week I worked happily within a large open window, with plenty of scope either to try harder or to relax a little. Now, with so little sleep, the window is a faint crack, if there at all. I feel I'm wasting this precious opportunity for practice by just fighting off sleep. I've come here to work with Tipun's question: 'What is the difference between the mind resting in tranquillity and the mind moving in thought?', and so far I have met not a moment's tranquillity.

I'm feeble and a failure. I imagine there must be some really good reason for sleep deprivation, and that I'm entirely fooling myself that there's any value in the work I did last week, because real monks and serious Buddhists know that true insight comes from breaking down the mind in exhaustion. In this case I must try harder. But I can't. I'm too tired. Then I reflect that maybe that's wrong, and I should have more confidence in what I've learned on my own. And so I go on, enduring the sleepiness, staggering through one hour after the next, accepting that I'm just a beginner and must plod on.

This morning in the yard, John said, 'It is not meant to be a penance here at the Maenllwyd. Enjoy!' It is a penance. I'm not enjoying it.

But I've got a new job! Whoever was assigned to look after the toilets apparently could not cope, and John knows that I can. So I am back to looking after the twin-vault, urine-separating, composting toilets, in solitude and silence; checking the pipes, washing the seats, mopping the floor and watching each square of the tiles come clean.

At breakfast, when we're all chanting the short grace that precedes each meal, I suddenly notice something I've never noticed before. We chant 'At one with the food, we identify with the universe.' I know what that means now. That's what I was doing last week – throwing myself out into the world and being the universe rather than being someone observing the universe. I plod on, just slightly encouraged.

Now we are all given copies of those old familiar pages from Tipun's notebook, and I am longing to get into the questions, but I realise, with some surprise, that there is a lot else in these pages apart from the questions that so fascinated me, and John is clearly going to concentrate on other things entirely. This morning his daily talk is all about life as a string of beads.

The text explains that 'Life appears to be an endless sequence of thoughts, feelings, happenings', and suggests that we ask ourselves, 'Is it not so?' The next task is to look into the beads so that they begin to become transparent in order to see what was not previously observed – i.e. the string. This unobserved string is also described as 'pure pristine cognition'.

Obediently, I ask myself 'Is it not so?' and I suppose it is. This is how life normally appears; as an endless sequence. This is William James's 'stream of thought, of consciousness, or of subjective life'. This is Antonio Damasio's 'movie in the brain'. This is the show in Dan Dennett's 'Cartesian theatre'. The difference between these thinkers is that for James and Damasio, the stream or movie is what a science of consciousness must explain. But for Dennett, this is all wrong, because neither the show nor the audience can be found in the brain and the brain is the only real place there is to look for them. So, on Dennett's view, whatever our science needs to explain, it is not this. I am firmly on Dennett's side after all this practice, and presumably on Tipun's. Yes, life starts out appearing as an endless sequence of thoughts, feelings and happenings, but what is it really? A lot of beads? On a string?

I use my next hour's meditation to look into the metaphor and conclude that it is not a good one. The beads are not lined up on a string at all because they are not happening one after the other, in one-dimensional time, to a single person. This was obvious to me all last week at home, when I was asking, 'What was I conscious of a moment ago?' I found whole streams of experience that seemed to have already been going on, for someone, before I noticed them – the birds singing in the garden, the builders hammering next door, the hum of the distant traffic on the Gloucester Road.

So I practise this again; this time with noisy sheep, and fidgeting people, and the crackling of the fire. These threads don't happen one after the other, but pop up all over the time and place, bringing with them their own sense of time and space, and their own observer. Seeing this, I let go of the notion of a central experiencing me and let the many streams arise and fall away, their observers coming and going with them. The question that naturally arises then is, where are they all coming from and going to? This becomes the inquiry.

So this is how it seems, not like a single string at all. Instead there is the whatever-it-is out of which all the multiple threads of experience come. I guess Tipun was asking us, 'Is it not so?' just to make us look.

Another hour comes and goes. I start seriously looking. I'm still sleepy; still struggling, but I have a go. Somehow, as I stare into where things are coming from, I seem to be pressed up against the world. This is the best way I can describe it. I know that I am not other than the experiences and so I throw myself into each one. Then in some peculiar way I seem to come up against them directly. It is as though 'I' am following the contours of the world out there. I am right up against it all.

This is very odd because it is not easy to see what it might mean to be pressed up against the contours of the evening fire flickering away against the dark grate, or the sudden call of the kite, or the smell of incense, or the chirruping of the blue tit outside the meditation hall. Nevertheless that is the best description I can give. And what is pressed up against all this? Emptiness of course. It is this space in which there is no existence, this whatever-it-is out of which everything comes which seems also to be me. There's something mirror-like about it, and I can see why that analogy is used, but mirrors are flat and this is not. It is as though I am the contours of the world.

In a moment of speculation, I wonder whether this is anything to do with that strange Zen notion of 'original face'. This derives from that koan I've heard so often but never worked with myself, 'What did your face look like before your parents were born?' Perhaps I'm reminded of this because it feels as though my own face is pressing up against the ever changing contours of the world. I also wonder what this has to do with the 'pure pristine cognition', because that's what I'm supposed to be looking into. Is this empty, black, alive and limitless self who is pressed up against the world a pristine knowing? I'm not even sure what 'pristine' means; something like 'clean' or 'clear' I suppose. I keep practising with this view and thinking about the beads and something seems to be happening. I can always ask John.

I get my chance next day, when we all have interviews. These are the informal sort, not a formal Zen interview with prescribed actions and inquiries. So John and I just sit comfortably and chat about how I got on last week, and how tough I'm finding it here.

At the end I ask him 'Is the string the same as the original face?' He says 'Yes', so I'm encouraged to carry on.

Things are getting better. I'm learning how to play the system and use every break to sleep. I manage to pack in three half-hour sleeps during the day, and I really do sleep; straight into that delicious, indescribable, falling feeling, and then awake from vivid multi-layered dreams, and back to work. I can even enjoy the rituals with their crazy visualisations of complicated deities, and their multiple aspects of wisdom, compassion and love. I am well aware that the insight or wisdom side of practice comes a lot more naturally to me than compassion, but I do start to see how they are related. We are told to think of compassion as 'empathising with the sorrows of others' and love as 'empathising with the joys of others', and this really strikes me. Oddly enough, it gets put to work almost straight away.

We are performing an invocation which involves not only chanting, but a lot of bashing on drums and blowing of horns (and no, I don't believe there's any entity out there to invoke). John even has a Tibetan horn made from a human thigh bone which makes a ghastly, mournful sound. One of the other women is given the cymbals to play and I'm jealous. I want to bash them and have fun making that lovely noise myself. But I remember the idea of 'empathising with the joys of others', and suddenly I find I'm enjoying her obvious delight in what she's doing, and I'm not jealous at all.

By evening I'm at last calm enough to work on the question: comparing the abiding mind with the mind moving in thought. As usual, I begin by letting the mind settle enough to see the thoughts arising out of the stillness. I then ask how they differ, when suddenly I notice something terribly obvious. In fact I have often noticed it before, but not seen its significance. That is, that by the time you catch those troublesome thoughts they seem already to have been going on for some time. This has always annoyed me, and my strategy has been to return to stillness and try to watch ever more carefully in the hope that I would be able to see them as soon as they appeared – to catch them starting up. I had assumed that the trick must be to be mindful enough, and open enough, so that everything that happens is caught instantly, and observed from the start, as it comes into awareness.

Now I take a completely different approach. Aha – of course – the thoughts are exactly like perceptions in this respect; they are like the crackling of the fire, the drifting incense smoke, or the bleating of sheep. By the time you notice them they have already been going on for some time, and it feels as though someone has been thinking them. Who is this someone? Seeing it this way means that I can apply the same strategy with thoughts as I did all last week with perceptions. In fact it had occurred to me then to try to do this with thoughts but I was unable, or perhaps unsure enough of its value, to persevere when everything seemed too quick and confusing. But now, with a slower mind, it's obvious that this is the path to take.

The first step, taking my cue from the perceptions, is to see that I am the thoughts.

I'm startled. I'm so startled that I just sit there in a startled state.

I remember the instruction to remain in non-elaboration, and so I just sit with this for a time without elaborating. What I have seen has the definite quality of insight. It occurs to me that this insight has arisen unbidden and I don't know what it means. Therefore I must sit with it and see, which I do. This makes sense of the fact that Tipun's text says 'to recognise and experience insight' in that order, which had seemed odd before. I had assumed you had to experience it first and then recognise it. But no, it's the other way around. The insight comes in a flash. Then you have to sit quietly with it and absorb the new view it provides. I sit in the experience of non-elaboration.

Some time later I begin to unravel just why the thought 'I am the thoughts' seems so startling. I think of William James and his famous claim that '*thought is itself the thinker*, and psychology need not look beyond'. I have read it, taught it to students, and written about it, countless times but must never have understood what he meant until now. It really is a radical move. It's extraordinary that he realised this in the late nineteenth century, presumably with no help from meditation.

This idea, that there is no thinker other than the thoughts, is startlingly counter-intuitive. In all my years of practising meditation I have always imagined either that I am the thinker of the thoughts (and I must stop thinking), or that the thoughts are memes that come to me from elsewhere (and I must ignore them). So I've always treated thoughts as a problem, or something to be dealt with. Now, instead of either fighting or watching them, I am simply to *be* them.

There's more. Taking my previous practice with perceptions, and applying it to thoughts, I can do the following: notice a thought, recognise that it has already been going on for some time, accept that I am both thought and thinker and have been for some time, allow them to be, and allow them to go. This keeps me busy. Another couple of sessions go by and make 'remaining in the experience of non-elaboration' quite natural.

Incidentally, I see that this answers Tipun's question: There is no difference between the mind moving in thought and the mind resting in tranquillity. But I doubt this is in any sense a final answer. I wonder whether the question 'How do thoughts arise?' is the same kind of trick. You are not supposed to find out because you cannot, but the process of looking provides insight, and so long as you don't know the answer, you keep looking.

There is frost tonight, and a nearly full moon.

It's the last full day and I can feel a cold coming on. So once again I'm finding it hard to sit.

In his morning talk John tells the story of the Dzogchen teacher, Patrul Rinpoche, and his monk, Nyoshul Lungtok. In a hermitage high above their monastery, the teacher asked his disciple to lie down on the ground and look up at the sky with him. 'Do you hear the dogs barking in the monastery?' asked the teacher, 'Do you see the stars shining in the sky? Well that's it!' he said. And in this moment Lungtok was enlightened.

John explains this story, saying that the monk had to be right there 'in the presence of the present moment', and that this way he could discover the 'awareness of awareness'. But to me the story suggests an utterly different interpretation. The examples of the dogs and stars are exactly the kind of thing that I have been calling the 'backwards threads'. I imagine that the monk, lying there on the grass with the great sky above, in the instant of having his attention drawn to the dogs, would have experienced two things simultaneously. One, he would feel as though he had only just become aware of the dogs barking, and two, he would realise that in some odd way he – or someone, or something – had been listening to the dogs all along. He would wonder who was hearing, and thus throw off the illusion of a permanent self.

The ordinary way in which people describe such experiences revolves around a continuing self; something like this: here 'I' am paying attention to the sky and the feel of the grass on my back, when suddenly 'my' attention shifts to the dogs barking; the barking was not previously 'in my consciousness' but now it is. The fact that it seems to have been experienced all along is usually ignored, or else is accounted for by saying that some unconscious part of the brain was noticing it, but now it has come 'into consciousness'. This interpretation requires two deeply troublesome ideas: first, the self who is conscious, and second, the idea that things can be either in or out of consciousness.

I have been trying to do without these. That's why I explored the backwards threads again and again and again, both in meditation and in mindful activity. Eventually my practice comes down to this: notice the new thread and its observer, accept that this new experience is me and allow it to arise and pass away, let go of any previous threads with their observers, and so on. There can be several of these happening at once. There is nowhere to find a foothold.

The difficult part, in my experience, is the letting go, but then it always is. This practice has a very odd quality about it. Self seems to dissolve into the multiple threads so that there is no longer any central self whose attention switches to one stream or another. So there is no longer a 'string of beads', or a 'stream of consciousness', or a 'movie in the brain', but experiences and experiencers that co-emerge all over the place and not to anyone in particular. It's much more like Dennett's 'multiple drafts'.

It's tempting to grab onto a central self who is in the middle of all this, but with practice it gets easier to ignore this powerful pull and just keep on letting go. The miraculous thing is that the physical body seems to carry on fine, while the experiencing selves just arise and fall away – with no one in charge.

This process takes quite a lot of describing, perhaps giving the impression that it is a terribly intellectual exercise, but it's not. It began from an intellectual decision, but that was just the motivation. The practice itself is a series of inner moves that I tried out, and just kept on and on trying until they came easily. After a while they had the effect of doing away with the sensation of being a central experiencing self who exists in any particular place or time.

Now I'm wondering where John's interpretation fits in. 'In the presence of the present moment' requires a 'present moment' and I have now lost this. I can easily get it back; it's always possible to construct a 'now' by tying together a few threads and sitting in the middle of them, but that's all it is – a construction – a kind of grabbing of a moment and calling it now. Better, I think, to reach out and realise that there was another you listening to the birds outside that had been going along at what would count as the same time from the perspective of that artificial 'now'. It is all a question of perspectives and there seem to be multiple perspectives all over the place and time, not one single viewing self who is 'here, now'.

Thinking this over, I wonder whether I am at fault because I have never really achieved full mindfulness, and that with much, much, more practice I might become so present and so open that there would be no more threads to find and I would really enter the 'now'. Maybe this is how the monk was supposed to be. I may well explore this in the future (one thing at a time!). But for now I have judged this implausible because it seems that unless you are dead there are always more threads.

What then of the 'awareness of awareness'? I can make no sense of this. Within the experiences I have described above there is, of course, a lurking mystery. Where do they all come from? I think I have a long way to go with this one, but so far my glimpses seem to be of a void out of which the threads are endlessly coming and going. They do not come and go out of a particular place and time – not just because their origin is invisible, but because place and time are intrinsic to them and come and go with them. So there is this bizarre sense that they are appearing and disappearing in and out of no place and no time – out there somewhere a world of bird song – oh, and while I'm about it a stove over there has long been crackling in the corner – and the hands are still there, as ever – and … but not in order, not comparable with each other, not in the same unitary four-dimensional space and time, just emerging out of … um?

This whatever-it-is does not seem well described by the phrase 'awareness of awareness'. It seems more like a void or an emptiness or a vast space of possibilities, while 'awareness of awareness' conjures up the idea of a super-ordinate awareness raising itself up over the previous one; exactly the reverse of what I had found.

I write my name on the board to request an interview with John.

Perhaps I am too challenging or aggressive – but then I'm excited. I want to understand. I want to know about the monk and what the story really means. So I try to explain why I think John's interpretation is wrong.

John listens attentively, and then gives his opinion: I am technically correct but I think too much and use too many words (and how many times have I been told that before!).

I try again, but he seems exasperated by my insistence that it is this way, and tries to press me with a simple question.

'For example', he says, 'are you, Sue, right now here in this room?'

'No', I reply. Of course I'm not. I haven't been through all of this only to end up still feeling as though I am some kind of conscious person sitting here at some location in time and space in this room now. It just isn't like that any more. I am so used to noticing the threads and letting one self go into any of a few other selves and dropping them too and letting the whole thing flow as it will, that I cannot truthfully say 'Yes'.

John says I must be. So I try to explain: I say that there is no 'right now' unless I make one up, and the general answer has to be 'no'.

He keeps arguing and there seems to me no point in pushing it. I am clear in my own mind that I'm only telling the truth. So I stand up, bow deeply, and walk to the door.

As my foot hits the first step he calls 'Stay'.

I turn and go back. We talk the whole thing through more carefully, and agree to differ. He gives me a 'red-flag' warning not to think too much, and I am sure this is good advice. I tell him I will follow his advice and keep working at the non-elaboration, as indeed I am doing. I must admit I am left perplexed.

I know that I think a lot and that this is frowned upon in tra-ditional Zen. Yet it seems to me that this is just one way of going about the task, and a way that suits me. The real test is whether the view at the end of the process is clearer than the view at the start. I think it is – and John said it was 'technically correct'. If it is, then the scaffolding used to get to it can safely be left behind. And surely it cannot matter whether it was an intellectual scaffolding or some other kind. Once it is left behind it won't be needed again and it need not cloud the view.

This encounter stirs my mind up rather, but it settles again, and that evening I write in my diary, 'everything simultaneously falling away as it is arising – coming up to meet me face to face but always meeting a different me, or maybe all just coming up out of? … I'll keep at it for the little while left.' And so I do.

On the drive home I discover something completely new. I decide to concentrate on my driving and to practise the trick I've been doing for so much of the last two weeks, of noticing and letting go the backwards threads; only this time they are the whine of the engine, the sound of the wind rushing past, and the sight of my arms emerging out of nowhere onto the steering wheel. The effect is that I am driving along in silence with everything arising all around and absolutely no thoughts.

I remember that a week ago I wondered whether it was really possible to have no thoughts. I decided that it might be but I couldn't see how you could tell you were having no thoughts with-out having the thought 'Am I thinking now?' Now I am driving without thinking while simultaneously observing the not thinking. I call this 'listening to the silence' although it doesn't seem a perfect name: something like listening to the silent space out of which the threads come. This nowhere becomes gradually more and more obvious.

If anyone had asked me 'Are you, Sue, right now here in this car?' I would have had to say 'No'.

9

What am I doing?

I am sitting outside my hut. It's summer now, and warm enough to put my mat and stool on the flagstones and sit outside, just in front of the flower bed.

A blackbird is singing on the garage roof; another answers from behind me somewhere. There are lots of birds singing, now I come to notice them, and even a seagull shrieking far above. 'Bristol isn't far from the sea and the gulls' ... let it go. The buzzing from countless bees and flies, messing about in the flowers, maps out a sonic space around me. The sun feels warm on my arms. I am sitting perfectly still: the mind is calming down.

I wonder what I'm doing here. Have I chosen to be here in just this spot, sitting just like this, of my own free will? How much of this am I doing, and how much is just happening to me? When I'm ready I will look into what it means to act.

What am I doing? I am sitting. That is, this body has been sitting here a long time. But does that really count as me doing it?

I am breathing. Yes, but the breaths go in and out whether I will them to or not. I can watch, or not, I can decide to breathe faster or hold my breath. But right now the breaths just come and go. No one is doing them.

I am hearing the birdsong and the bees. Yes, but I can't not hear them, and it feels quite passive. The sounds arise and fall away. I'm not making an effort to listen to them and I don't respond to them now that my mind has settled. So does that count as me doing it?

This is a strange question. Asking what I am doing seems to freeze me in a moment of not doing; of asking and not knowing the answer. I *was* asking the question but now … ?

I sit, not doing, and wonder. What am I doing?

I could do something else if I chose to, couldn't I? Ah yes, it seems so. This is the essence of having free will, and without that there would be no point in doing anything at all, would there?

I am sitting perfectly still, as I am supposed to in meditation. But if I wanted to I could lift one hand, or clap loudly, or ring the bell, or get up and walk away, or run out into the road shouting, 'I'm free. I can do anything I like!'

OK, I'll clap.

Clap.

Did I do that freely – for no other reason than that I consciously decided to do it?

Probably not. I thought of clapping because I was asking, 'What am I doing?' and casting around for something to do, and there aren't that many things you can easily do while sitting in meditation posture, and anyway clapping has a lot of history in Zen, so it's probably a likely candidate to be chosen by this brain at this time, and anyway, all of this goes back to why I'm sitting here this morning, and that goes back to …

OK. OK. I give up. I can trace back myriad possible reasons why this happened. But even so, in ordinary language, I would say that I did the clapping, not just that this body did it. Did I really? And if so, did I do it of my own free will?

I'm being too intellectual about this, and perhaps that's not surprising. Free will is said to be the most argued-about philosophical problem of all time, and I've read quite a lot of the philosophy.

The basic problem has been apparent for thousands of years both in Western philosophy and in Buddhism. The universe seems to be causally closed. That is, everything that happens is caused by something else. Nothing happens by magical forces intervening from outside the web of causes and effects, for everything is interconnected with everything else.

This means there is no sense to the idea of free will: no sense to the idea that I can jump in and consciously decide to do something without any prior causes, just because I want to. If that happened, it would be magic, implying that conscious actions lie outside the physical web of interconnectedness. Yet I feel as though I can act freely. Indeed this magical view is probably how most people in most cultures have always thought about themselves, imagining a non-physical mental entity that has wishes and desires, can think and plan, and can carry out those plans by acting on the world. But non-physical things cannot act in the physical world without magic, and the more we learn about how the brain works, the less room there is for magical interventions by conscious minds. We are back to dualism and the problem that Descartes never solved, and no one else has since.

In Zen, and in the languages in which early Buddhist texts were written, there is no equivalent of the Western concept of free will, but there is plenty about doing and not-doing. On his enlightenment, the Buddha is said to have awakened to the realisation that all phenomena in all times co-arise in an interconnected web of cause and effect. This is known as 'dependent origination' or 'dependent co-arising'. Everything is part of everything else: nothing has its own self-nature, independent of the rest, including people. If this is so, then no one can be said to act independently of everything else, hence 'Actions exist, and also their consequences, but the person that acts does not.' In its completely different way, Buddhism is saying the same as science – however it feels, there's no room for magical interventions.

To resolve the problem of free will philosophers have come up with all sorts of ways of recasting the problem; for example by treating actions and choices as free if they are not forced, and finding ways in which free action can be compatible with determinism, but I want to stick with the ordinary, everyday sense of the phrase 'free will.' That is, the sense in which it feels as though 'I' have consciously caused things to happen. In that sense the solution seems, purely intellectually, to be obvious. There cannot be free will. It doesn't make sense.

So what to do? Many people come to a similar conclusion and then say, 'But I cannot live my life not believing in free will, so I will just act "as if" there's free will.' And that seems to satisfy them.

It does not satisfy me. I am not prepared to live my life pretending the world is otherwise than it is. So I have worked hard at this one, systematically challenging the feeling of having free will whenever it arises. Now it rarely catches me out and actions seem to happen on their own. Even so, there is always room for deeper inquiry, and so it was with some enthusiasm that I set aside the time to investigate what it's like to act, and decide, and do.

I am sitting outside my hut, and the morning air is fresh and chilly, even though it's mid-summer. The flowers of the feverfew in front of me are back-lit by the early morning sun: small and white with tiny yellow centres. I am calming the mind for half an hour before I start work on today's question. One cat sits beside me; the other on a chair across the orchard. Out of the corner of my eye I see something move, something cat-like though rather large. But both my cats are here. 'Let …'

What is it?

I cannot, or do not, resist. I turn my eyes to look.

A fox slips quietly between them.

I shouldn't have done that. I am supposed to keep looking straight down at the flowers and grass. Was that free will? Surely not. The movement of the fox and my own curiosity made me do it. Er? 'My' curiosity. Was this me doing it?

Not yet. I go back to sitting quietly, but thoughts start bubbling up; the foxes all died out in Bristol a few years ago and now they've just begun to come … 'Let …'

There you are, you see. I did that, didn't I? It was me who jumped in with 'Let it go …', and the thoughts went away. But I know immediately that this isn't true. I learnt that trick from

John all those decades ago. That meme, those words 'Let it come. Let it be. Let it go', is one he infected me with when I first started meditating, and it's been working away in my mind ever since. But then I choose to keep it rather than forget it, or reject it, or tell myself it's stupid, or any number of other things I might have done. So it is up to me that I keep on using the trick, isn't it?

No, not really. The reasons for rejection or acceptance are my personality, my genetic make-up, other memes I've picked up along the way, and force of circumstance. All this has led to a person who sits here now, and when the thoughts start rattling away whispers 'Le ...', and they stop.

So where do I come into this? It's all bound up with me. For me to have free will means that I do something of my own accord. So who am I?

Ah. That's a familiar one. I'll sit and see who is here for a bit. Perhaps then I will be able to see if she's doing anything.

Here it is; the headless body topped with grass and pretty white flowers. It sits still.

Do I have free will? I hear the words. I ask. I am stumped.

Perhaps I need to work with something easier, with the absolute minimal requirement for free will, which is that I actually do things. I must go back to the simple question.

What am I doing?

I can sit with that. I can stay calm and clear and ask, 'What am I doing?'

I sit. The buzzing continues; the cats do not stir.

I am sitting up straight. But it's not exactly me who's doing this. It's such a long-practised habit that this body just gets into that position and stays there. Maybe it makes sense to say that my body is doing it; but am 'I' doing it?

All right then, I'm making an effort here. I'm paying attention. That really is an effort. Indeed, that is the whole task of meditation; that you have to stay there, minute after minute, hour after hour, and keep on paying attention, not sliding off, not getting sidetracked into worries, or fantasies, or imagined conversations. You have to work at paying attention. I am paying attention right now. And now.

So that's the key isn't it? If I didn't make the effort then it wouldn't happen. It's an effort of will; it's hard work. I am using my own will to pay attention, now and now, and keeping on paying attention. It's hard work. So this is what I am doing. The hard work, and the effort I feel myself making, are proof that I'm doing something.

But oddly enough, I realise, hard work doesn't prove anything of the kind. As I sit here, I remember the birth of my first child, many years ago. She had a very big head, or something else wasn't quite right, and I was in labour for more than 24 hours. It was terribly hard work and terribly painful. That's why it's called 'labour', I realised. And who was making the effort? I had this extraordinary sense that I was doing the hard work, but that I had no option. I couldn't say 'No. I don't want to have this baby. I won't do it.' My body was doing it all of its self. I was doing the hardest physical work I had ever done in my life, and yet I was not willing it. The labour was willing itself. Doing, and yet not doing.

Come back now, back to the garden, sit calmly, pay attention.

Hard work does not prove that it's a matter of will, or that I am doing it. So what am I doing?

I am sitting still again. I can see the taller flowers, pink behind the white, and the branches of an apple tree moving in the chilly breeze. I feel the wind.

Am I doing this? Am I looking at them and seeing them? Is seeing doing?

Yes, but I couldn't do it without them. They are as much doing it as I am. Which is moving – me or them? Is the moving in my mind or in the world out there?

The trick of turning inwards unfolds itself again. There are the flowers, then legs and arms, and half a nose, and then where there should be me inside there are only the moving flowers and apple branches. I am not doing this. It's all of a piece. The looking, the seeing, the moving, we're doing it together. It's just stuff happening; the universe doing its thing. The body goes on sitting still. The branches keep on waving.

Nine o'clock strikes. End of meditation. She bows. She gets up. Did I do that?

I am feeling strange. I am used to these mental manoeuvres, yet they still have a deep effect.

I get up and walk attentively, without assuming that I'm doing anything. The legs are walking, the grass and flowerbed are slipping by in the space where I should be.

There are raspberries to be picked for breakfast. A hand

reaches out, and again, and again. It can choose this bush or that one. It picks this one, until enough are picked. It's time to go indoors, but which way will she go?

I like making paths, and there are several quite unnecessarily bendy and pointless paths in our garden. In fact there are three ways I can go, one with low branches to duck under, another narrowed by spreading weeds, and the last clear but longer. Which way shall I go? I try to catch myself in the act of making the decision. Everything slows down horribly, I stand hovering with one foot raised, to see whether I can catch my own mind making itself up. If I could catch this moment, or watch this process, I might find out what it's like to act freely, and to know that I am really doing this. A hand reaches out to a just-noticed ripe raspberry, the cats suddenly scamper past, on their way into the house, and a foot is already following them. They go to the place on the wall where I always stroke them before going indoors. The hand reaches out, the fur is soft and the cat's head presses against the hand.

So she must have decided to go that way.

This seems to be all that happens; decisions are made because of countless interacting events, and afterwards a little voice inside says 'I did that', 'I decided to do that'.

Is there any need for that little, after-the-fact, voice?

I must watch some more.

Do I have free will?

No. I am not separate from the perceptions, thoughts and actions that make up my world. And if I am what seems to be the world, then we are in this together. Me and the world, world/me are doing all these actions that now just seem to act of their own accord.

But help!

Help. Surely this means that I am not responsible. This is terrible. If I'm not responsible then ...

My mind goes back many years to when I was first practising mindfulness, and hit upon this fear. We were staying at a campsite in Austria, by a lake, and I was on a little beach with the children. It was a lovely day, and the place was quite peaceful except for a blaring radio. It was very annoying.

I knew what I would usually do in such circumstances. I would fret. I would be angry, I would think about the regulations of the campsite, think about telling him to turn it off, feel bad at the thought of doing so, look at his tattoos and worry what he'd do if I approached him, think that if I were a real Buddhist I would feel compassion rather than anger, imagine that if I were a good meditator I wouldn't mind the noise, try not to mind, fail. And so on.

So what did happen? Many such thoughts began but each was met with 'Let ...' and fizzled out, leaving the grass before my feet, the mud pies the children were making, the feel of the earth on my hands as I joined in, the sounds of birds, the sounds of the radio, the grass again as I walked up the beach and stopped, my voice (this time in the best German I could manage) saying, 'Excuse me, your radio is very loud, would you please mind turning it down?', the man's face scowling and muttering, his hand reaching out to his radio, the grass and then the mud and stones rough under my feet, and the mud pies and children.

Some time later I noticed that he had gone. I began to wonder whether I'd done the 'right thing' or not, but 'Let ...' and back to the feel of the water on my toes. A brief moment's thought was quite enough to realise that agonising about what to do would not have helped. The world had summed up the options, chosen one, carried it out, and moved on. This action was a result of everything I had learned and done before. It was long past. Now was, as ever, fine. And now.

Deep breath. Watch again. The world said, 'Deep breath, watch again.' This perfectly sensible response was not coming from a little thing inside called 'me'; it came from somewhere, I don't know where, from all the past actions of this body, and this brain, and everything it's gone through. It just happened. It's OK. There's nothing wrong with that response.

So is it always like this? Could I just trust the world and this body to work all by itself without me doing anything? I realise with a certain horror that by relinquishing myself to the world, and accepting that actions just happen, I have given up all personal responsibility. It's gone. I cannot believe in it any more. There's no one in here making the decisions. They are making themselves. I have just walked in from the hut, fed the cats, had breakfast, and made loads of little decisions along the way, all with alert attention to what's happening, and with no sense of myself doing it.

It seems so right. It seems truthful to the way things really are.

But what about responsibility?

I have played around with this question intellectually since my teens, when I first worked out that free will must be an illusion, but it was only after many years of meditating that I confronted the problem directly.

I was on a Zen retreat at Maenllwyd and practising intensely. Our teacher for the week was Reb Anderson, a Zen master visiting from California, and he was pushing us hard. As the illusion of doing began to loosen its grip, I became frightened. The world was seeping into me and I was disintegrating into the world. I was acting and not acting. This flowing sense of action without an actor felt perfectly natural, but as soon as I started thinking about it I hit the problem. Help! – what about responsibility? There could be none in such a world.

I signed up for an interview. The Zen master was an impressive and good-looking man, with shaven head and imposing robes, and this was a formal interview. I walked steadily to the interview room, opened the door quietly and slipped in. I bowed in the prescribed way, sat in the prescribed posture, looked straight into his shining eyes, and plucked up the courage to tell him what I thought: that ultimately no one is responsible for anything.

He chuckled.

'Yes', he said with a delightfully warm and encouraging smile, '*ultimately,* that's true.' He seemed to emphasise the 'ultimately', and I thought of the Zen distinction between the ultimate view and the relative view, wondering whether there's some other way in which it's not true.

'Then what do I do about responsibility?' I blurted out.

'You *take* responsibility', he said.[1]

Help, help, and again help. Who takes responsibility? Isn't 'taking responsibility' doing something? Isn't taking responsibility an act of will? Doesn't it require someone who is doing it? Isn't it freely done? No, in this case he had told me to do it, so it wasn't free. But I could refuse to do it …

Then who would refuse to do it? I know there is no entity inside here called myself, so isn't taking responsibility just inventing a new false self who is going to have that responsibility? Why would one want to do that if one knew that there really was no self?

I am going round in circles. Help.

Gradually over the years, as the sense of having free will has slipped away, I have remembered this advice and it has helped.

The illusion of free will does not survive the kind of scrutiny I have given it here. It simply melts away. I no longer even feel its pull. People sometimes ask me how I did it; how I gave up free will, but I cannot tell them. I know that I battled intellectually with it for years, but thinking only creates a mismatch between what one intellectually believes and how the world seems to be. I never felt comfortable with this mismatch, and didn't want to go on living as though free will were true when logic and science told me it could not be. I didn't want to live a lie, or a half-truth, or an 'as if'. So this great intellectual doubt drove me to look directly into how decisions are made, and on to examine the self which ultimately underlies the feeling of being someone who freely acts.

I no longer get that feeling. Just sometimes a pale shadow of it rises up – 'Oh help, I've got to decide what to wear for my lecture this evening', or 'I don't know whether to accept this work offer or turn it down.' I welcome these as a chance to look again, to investigate what it feels like to make a conscious decision, but all the habits of paying attention and watching what happens dissipate the feeling very quickly. It has nothing to cling to.

So it works something like this. An email arrives. It's a wonderful invitation to give a lecture in an exciting far-away place, at a prestigious conference with all expenses paid. I look in my diary. That day I've agreed to go with my partner to a family event I know he'd love me to attend. It's been planned for ages. What to do? I have to decide. I'm a reliable person. I don't like letting anyone down. The lecture is a terrific opportunity. It won't come again. But I've already committed myself.

No, 'I' don't have to decide. There is no inner me who can do so. This whole series of events is part of the play of the world/me as it is, and the decision is too. So the thoughts come, and the feelings of indecision come, and the feelings sway back and forth, and the weighing-up goes on, and it's all just stuff happening, like the cars going by and the ticking of the clock in the background. Then the decision somehow is made, whether it's today or three days later. Eventually the fingers type the replying email and it's done. And then what?

Then I take responsibility. I don't mean that a little inner me who has free will does so, because that would be to fall back into the endless cycle of the illusion of doing. The little me is a fiction. I mean only that consequences will follow and I will accept them. If someone tells me how wonderful the conference was and I missed it I won't be angry that 'I' made the wrong decision. It was made. That's what happened and that's how it is now. If someone is cross with me for being so selfish and mean for not joining the family event I will accept that punishment. That's what happened, these are the consequences. Things just are the way they are. Whether they could have been different I do not know, but I suspect that even asking this question does not make sense. Stuff just happens.

Indeed the fingers are typing here right now. No one is acting. I am not doing anything.

What, then, is the point of it all? What's the point in doing anything?

No point.

---

[1] Years later, I met Reb again and we talked about doing and not doing. He said that his suggestion to 'take responsibility' had become a kind of koan for me, which I had struggled with. Now, he says, he would probably say 'accept responsibility – without limit.'

10

What happens next?

Will I be reborn? Will I live after my body has died? Will I go to heaven, or hell, or anywhere? Or will my consciousness just be snuffed out like a candle? Gone? Dead? That's it?

At the heart of this question lies the great question of self: Who am I? For surely if I know who or what I really am, then I might see the answer. But I have had enough experience of looking for my self to know that I am not going to find it. I have looked into experiences to find the me who was experiencing them – and found only more experiences. I have asked whether I am the same me as I was a moment ago, and found I could not tell. I have looked into the centre of this experienced world and not found myself in the middle. I have looked into actions to find who is doing them, and found that no one is.

Why, then, does this question still seem worth asking?

I know why. It's because I want to survive. I want to be here when my children grow up. I want to see what happens. There is unquestionably something in me that wants to carry on. It might be childish, and selfish, but if I'm honest I have to admit it. I don't want to be snuffed out; not now, not when I die, not ever.

I suppose other people feel much the same, and that's why this question has caused so much trouble and disagreement between religions and science.

Science has no need of a spirit or a soul that inhabits the body. There is no room for one in the brain, and nothing for it to do if it were there. There is no need for an inner self to explain how we perceive things or how we act upon them. The body, brain and world are enough. Although science cannot rule out these supernatural possibilities, it has no need to invent them. From this perspective death certainly looks like snuffing out.

By contrast, most religions promise some kind of personal survival. Hindus believe that their soul will be reincarnated in a series of future lives. Christians and Muslims believe that their soul will go to heaven or hell when their physical body dies. Spiritualists believe they can contact the surviving spirits of the dead. Buddhism alone denies the existence of a soul or spirit. This is the whole point of the Buddha's insights into no-self and dependent co-arising. Yet many Buddhists, especially in the Tibetan tradition, believe in personal reincarnation. This is very confusing. But I am not going to get caught up with doctrinal differences. I want to look directly.

I have an inkling that those multiple threads I was exploring before might give me a clue; there's something peculiar about these backwards threads of things that seem already to have happened, or to have been happening to someone or something that wasn't me. I'll take another look.

Here I sit in my little hut. It is mid-winter and cold, but not raining for a change. I settle down. There is a lot going on. I sit with it and pay attention. I begin to notice the threads, one by one, more and more.

Here I am, thinking (in words) that it's time to clear the mind and settle down, when I notice the background hum of the distant traffic, and a car becoming louder and then fainter as it passes up the street. It feels as though while my intention was forming itself someone else was already listening to that car; hearing its rise and fall. Hmm. I sit. There are birds singing. Oh yes, I have been listening to them for some time now. I can remember that chirrupy little tune. They are mostly blackbirds, two of them, competing for territory, and some pigeons flying about in their noisy fashion. Someone was listening to all that too.

The loud bang of a hammer and the whine of a power drill intrudes but does not bother me. Someone has been listening to those builders' sounds too. But the cat sitting beside me is startled. She jumps, and settles down again. Yes, someone was aware of her being there, nestling in the rug. It's as though I can remember having felt her warmth there for some time, even though I also think I became aware of her only when she jumped.

This is what I am after. This is the paradoxical feeling that suggests a link with reincarnation. I want to look into this odd experience and see what is going on.

I set myself the following task.

Intellectually I do not believe that there is an inner self who is doing all this experiencing. Yet it still feels as though there is. I'm not prepared to live with this horrible clash between how it feels and how I think it must be, and I've done quite enough intellectual arguing. So now I'm going to look, and look, and look, and find out whether it really does seem, or always must seem, that there's a me who experiences the experiences, and is the same me as before, and is the same me who'll be here to see the future.

I sit and watch the threads. Ah, there's that road noise again; the birds are still singing in next door's garden; the builders are still crashing about. But something annoying is happening. I realise that when I look I'm still thinking in terms of a continuous me who becomes aware of each thread in turn: of a conscious self who notices first one thread and then another. But this is wrong. I must let go of that assumption and just watch. After all, it is the odd sense that someone had been listening to the birds all along that first gave me this clue – this determination to look into this more, and I'm not being true to it.

I try again. Watch and listen.

Now I'm, once again, getting used to that odd sense that some-one, not me, has been feeling my ankles on the floor; someone, not me, has been listening to the faint rustle of wind across the hedge; someone, not me, has been aware of the shadows on the grey stones. I begin to let go and allow there to be several simultaneous experiencers without flipping back into the ordinary view.

Yet something is still wrong. I seem to have replaced the old view with the idea that I am pulling the threads together in some way, and becoming aware of them all at once in a great mindful space. I'm still imagining a central me who is doing this. And I don't know whether this me is necessary or not. Perhaps I've just invented her to try to explain the oddity of it all. Perhaps I could do without her. But if so, where would I look from? What would remain?

I try to calm down. I notice that my breathing has paused and then quickened. It normally drops to a regular three breaths a minute during meditation, but there's something scary going on here and I am not sure what it is. Calm down, breathe gently, and look again.

What seems to be required is this … to allow each thread to arise, along with whoever is experiencing it, and then let both fall away again, without gathering them up into the 'real me' who was, or was not, conscious of the sound, touch or sight. This is a radical kind of letting go.

So – go on – do it.

I try. I try. Something holds me back from leaping into … what? a gap? a void? The opportunity comes and goes. I try again.

Yet I know that any kind of trying defeats the object of the exercise. By trying so hard I am invoking that very sense of a self that I am trying to do without. But if I don't try I'll never find out. So what to do? Not do?

I keep trying.

Then suddenly it's possible. Perhaps all those years of practising some kind of letting go have stood me in good stead. There goes the traffic noise, thrumming along. Someone has been listening to it all the time. Let it arise, let it be for however long it stays, and let it go. Meanwhile, in parallel with that, something else has risen up. The birds are singing. The drill has started up again.

There's a sense that each arises, stays for a while, and fizzles out. They're not being attended to one at a time, but go on in parallel with nothing holding them together.

It is the fizzling out that is the tricky bit. I notice that as each sound or feeling dies away, or ceases being brought into play, there is a bit of me that wants to hang on to it; that wants to keep saying, 'I experienced that. I remember it. I exist.' But the task is clear. Let all these threads do their stuff, and that includes fizzling out again. So they are let go. It is possible after all. They do just seem to arise and fall away again, but not to me.

I have a little chuckle. For years and years I have understood John's instruction to 'Let it come, let it be, let it go' in the following way. Here I am, being mindful, practising meditation, sitting in the middle of my world, and along comes some thought or idea or perception. What I must do is let it arise – here in my consciousness – let it be for a little while and then, when its time is up, let it go out of my consciousness again. I've done it for years, and very useful it has been too.

But now it seems that it isn't like that at all. No, not at all. Rather, there are myriad things arising and staying for a while being experienced by someone and then fizzling out again. The meaning of John's meme is to let that happen. It is not that they are happening to *me*. They are not coming, being and going, to *me*. It's all just happening anyway, whether I like it or not. The task is not to prevent it, not to interfere with it, not to suppose that there even is a me who could interfere with it all. Ah.

The traffic reappears and seems to have been there for some time. So do the birds. And the cat has decided to get up and walk out. A hand stretches out to stroke along her back as she passes by. The flagstone is still there, solidly stone-like, and today it is dry.

Why was it so difficult before? One answer is that I was struggling to grasp some kind of continuity. Long ago, when I first began paying attention, I noticed how discontinuous ordinary life is. I seemed to wake up and then get lost again; come to and be angry that I had been so far away. Everything was jerky and spasmodic and I didn't like it. I wanted to stay conscious, and be really me, all the time. This was one of the joys of learning to practise mindfulness. At last it seemed possible to gain some kind of continuity. In paying attention to what is here and now, right now, something kept going. It wasn't much. It came and went. But it was a kind of conscious continuity, and I welcomed it.

Am I now throwing all this away? Yes, indeed. I am exploring the possibility that actually I am not a continuous conscious being at all. 'I' am not that kind of thing. I am exploring the idea that what seems to be me just arises along with whatever is being experienced, and then fizzles out again when that experience comes to its natural end. This would fit with what I know of the way the brain works. It doesn't have a central processor that is in charge, nor any kind of command headquarters for me to sit in and issue edicts to the world, nor any space or place where consciousness happens. There are just multiple parallel pathways of neurons firing away all the time. So yes, I am throwing away the idea of continuity of self.

Isn't this scary? Yes, it is scary. On the one hand I still want to exist and to go on existing forever. I want to be the inner me who has lived all my life so far, who will go on living it, and who will see what happens next. But on the other hand I want to know the truth, and the idea of a conscious self just does not seem to be true, either in science or in experience. The facts seem, now, to be no more than this disparate coming and going, this selfless arising, being and passing away. It gets a little easier to sit with this.

So it goes on. Stuff is happening and I'm not getting in the way, and then the oddest thing happens.

What should come about but a sense of continuity? This is really strange. Sitting here, all these hours, letting threads come and go. Being one, being another, hanging on to none, being many at once, or none, and there is this sense of continuity.

What is it? What is continuing? It is not me, that's for sure. For every time some experience comes along, the me is allowed to go, along with the ending of the experience, as though experience and experiencer arise and then snuff out together. Nothing is held on to from one to the next.

So what is it? Perhaps the continuity is just that of the universe going on doing its stuff. Then there is no need to fear, for stuff will keep coming; selves having experiences will keep popping up, or not. Each one provides an opportunity for grasping, for taking it as the experience of a continuing self, but they needn't be taken this way.

Perhaps the continuity is that of the timeless, placeless emptiness, or void, or whatever it is, out of which phenomena appear. Then the same applies. There is no need to fear, for stuff will keep coming out of nothing, or not. Indeed, perhaps those two are one and the same.

Perhaps the sense of continuity is nothing more than this: the continuity of the whole universe. Funny that letting go of continuity should provide so rich a sense of it.

Now what does this have to do with birth and death, and rebirth, and whether I shall carry on after my body is dead? That niggling sense that the threads had something to do with it gave me a clue. And it's very simple. There never was a continuous I. There isn't now, there wasn't a moment ago, and there won't be in the future. Experiences and their experiencers will arise wherever and whenever there is a body capable of sensing things, and a brain capable of analysing them, and they will last some time and disappear again. They are now here, now there, coming and going. I seem to be here now, but then I'm not. Something else is, and has been for some time.

So being aware is always being born and dying again. There is nothing unusual in this. That's just how it is. When this body dies these particular sorts of experiences and experiencers will not arise any more. There will be no yellow flowers seen from quite this position with quite these eyes; no friendly beloved cat sitting at my side just here, because here will not exist any more; at least, not as it has, in similar fashion, so many times before. Were these times similar? Yes. Were they the same me? No. Every thread came about and then fizzled out. The 'same me' was never recreated.

When this body dies there may be a lot of pain, a horrible last illness, the sadness of not having said all those things I wanted to say to people I loved, projects not completed, a fantasised future not to be. But will I be snuffed out like a candle? Yes, just as I have been a thousand, million times before. Just the same. Being born and dying again is how all life is. Birth and death are not a problem; the cycle of illusion is broken; they are just how it is.

Being conscious

Consciousness is an illusion; an enticing and convincing illusion that lures us into believing that our minds are separate from our bodies. The illusion works so well that it has led the science of consciousness studies in completely the wrong direction; into grappling with the 'hard problem' instead of asking how the illusion of dualism is created.

According to most of today's scientists and philosophers, consciousness is equivalent to subjectivity: it is 'what it is like to be me'. So the 'hard problem' of consciousness is to explain how each person's private stream of subjective experiences is created by the objective structures and processes of the brain. This problem is hard – and some would say insoluble – because it implies that a physical brain creates non-physical experiences, and we know that this kind of dualism cannot be made to work. So what should we do?

There are plenty of scientists who doubt that we understand the brain well enough, and many who hope that once we do the problem will be solved. There are far fewer whose doubt extends to the 'what it's like to be me' that they are trying to explain. This is where my own doubts lay. So I looked very hard into what it's like to be me and I found no answer. The very thing that the science of consciousness is trying to explain, disintegrated on closer inspection.

When I stare into the face of arising experiences, I find that the whole idea of there being a me, a 'what it's like to be me now', and a stream of experiences I am having, falls apart.

It falls apart, first, because there is no persisting me to ask about. Whenever I look for one, there seems to be a me, but these selves are fleeting and temporary. They arise along with the sensations, perceptions and thoughts that they seem to be having, and die along with them. In any self-reflective moment I can say that I am experiencing this, or that, but with every new 'this' there is a new 'me' who was looking into it. A moment later that is gone and a different self, with a different perspective, pops up. When not reflecting on self, it is impossible to say whether there is anyone experiencing anything or not.

It falls apart, second, because there is no theatre of the mind in which conscious experiences happen. Experience, when examined closely, is not the show on our personal stage that the illusion has us imagine. Sensations, perceptions and thoughts come and go, sometimes in sequences but often in parallel. They are ephemeral scraps, lasting only so long as they are held in play, not unified and organised, not happening in definite times and places, not happening in order for a continuing observer. It is impossible to say which ones are, or were, 'in consciousness' and which not.

If this is so, then many of the traditional claims, relied upon in the field of consciousness studies, are false, and the theories and experimental paradigms that depend on them are correspondingly misguided. This has come about because it is so easy to rely upon the illusion, to look briefly into our own minds and assume that we know what they are like, and because introspection is so very difficult. But we will never make progress with a science of consciousness if we are trying to explain the wrong thing.

So I reject many of those common assumptions and would say instead the following:

> There is nothing it is like to be me.
> I am not a persisting conscious entity.
> I do not consciously cause the actions of my body.
> Consciousness is not a stream of experiences.
> Seeing entails no vivid mental pictures or movie in the brain.
> There is no unity of consciousness either in a given moment or through time.
> Brain activity is neither conscious nor unconscious.
> There are no contents of consciousness.
> There is no now.

I am not claiming to provide a coherent alternative, much less a new theory of consciousness, but here is my best attempt to describe what I think we should be trying to explain.

At any time in a human brain there are multiple parallel processes going on, conjuring up perceptions, thoughts, opinions, sensations and volitions. None of these is either in or out of consciousness for there is no such place. Most of the time there is no observer: if consciousness is involved at all it is an attribution made later, on the basis of remembering events and assuming that someone must have been experiencing them in the past, when in fact no one was.

Some of the time there are processes complex enough to

support an apparent observer as well. These observers arise with the thoughts and perceptions they seem to be having, and fall away again when they dissipate. So there is no persistent self, or viewpoint, from which events are observed. Indeed every such thought or perception is seen from a different viewpoint, but we falsely assume it is always the same one.

If we start to wonder about our own minds, or ask such questions as 'What is in my consciousness now?', or 'Who am I?', we construct an observing self and provide an answer, but most of our lives we are not going around asking such questions, or thinking about self. The mistake is to imagine that the answers we get at these special times apply to the rest of our experience. For the rest of the time there is no answer.

This means that instead of looking for the neural correlates of consciousness, the contents of consciousness, the global workspace, or Crick's 'consciousness neurons' we should be trying to understand how and why the brain pulls off these tricks and creates the illusion. We already know a great deal about how colours, shapes and objects are constructed, and about how actions are initiated and organised, and will doubtless learn much more. We do not also need to ask 'how do some of these become conscious?' because they do not.

Instead we need to examine those moments in which temporary observers are constructed and try to understand what is happening in the brain. I suspect that the processes involved entail a connection between sensory or motor processes, and verbal processes that construct a self. This would mean they cannot occur in animals that have no sense of self, or in machines that do not use natural language. In doing this we may also find out how constructing an apparent observer entails making a viewpoint from which events are seen and are ordered in time. Depending on where in the brain this is going on, different events will appear to happen simultaneously or in one order or another. This could help us understand why 'me' and 'now' emerge together.

Even more interesting will be to understand the basis of those special moments in which one asks 'Am I conscious now?' or 'Who am I?' I suspect that these entail a massive integration of processes all over the brain and a corresponding sense of richer awareness. These probably occur only rarely in most people, but contribute disproportionately to our idea of 'what it's like to be me'. This kind of rich self-awareness may happen more of the time, and more continuously, for those who practise mindfulness. Does it completely disappear in those who transcend it?

In writing about all this I have noticed that I sometimes seem to articulate ideas long before I fully understand them. Perhaps this is why Tipun's notebook refers to recognising insight before going on to experience it, although that does imply that we can tell insight from delusion. I remember a very long time ago, when smoking cannabis, concluding that 'You must learn to take the top layers off.' I had no idea what it meant, but I remembered it, kept practising it, and wrote it in my notebook. It felt right and I trusted that intuition. Decades later I think the top layers are all the temporary observers, theories about the world, and illusions of continuity and agency that brains so easily construct. When these are dropped, or a brain no longer constructs them, the world just bubbles up as it is.

In that state, experience seems much closer to what we know is happening inside the brain: there is no persisting self, no show in a mental theatre, no power of consciousness and no free will, no duality of self and other – just complex interactions between a body and the rest of the world, arising and falling away for no one in particular.

Response of a Zen master

After I had finished writing this book, I sent a draft copy to several friends, inviting comments or criticisms. This included John Crook, who I hoped might offer some comments as my Zen teacher.

He wrote back the following letter, with a p.s. inviting me to include it in the book if I wished. The first section includes two paragraphs about publishers, deadlines and endorsement, and I have deleted these. The rest is verbatim.

Thursday, July 5, 2007

Dear Sue,

Ten Zen Questions

Yesterday evening I read through your text fully for a second time. I came to more or less the same conclusions so I am now ready to write to you. I will have to telescope my reply because there is so very much one could say. Here are the leading comments and it will be fun to talk them over some time.

I reply in two ways – firstly as a response to the MS as such and then from my Zen teacher's perspective – as you asked me to do.

1. The MS

I found your book extremely well written, clear and provocative, characterised by the energy and intelligence that you apply to all your projects. To me, of course, it reads like an extended retreat report because so much of it is derived from your Zen 'apprenticeship' with me. I find your accounts of our retreats heart warming, precise and truthful. Your 'enquiry' into these questions is diligently carried out from a Zen perspective and you have made a number of interesting discoveries for yourself. This could only come about because of the intensity and application of the method – however, as we shall see below, the job in Zen terms is not complete – of course nothing is ever complete.

I will not comment much on your contribution to 'Consciousness studies' although I agree fully that 'subjective empiricism', as I called it in 1980,[1] is as fully relevant as 'objective empiricism' in the investigation of the conscious experiencing mind. In fact, you are continuing a tradition of Western phenomenological research but using a Zen methodology that no Western psychologist to my knowledge has applied to this problem.

In this part of my response, I am writing from a perspective of a Western psychologist. I am sure many colleagues will not understand you because they have no idea about Buddhist empiricism. …

2. A Zen perspective

What follows is a response to your saying that you are continuing with your Zen practice and enquiry. There is much to say and I must limit it to the main points. I have put my 'Zen hat' on.

i. In defining your focus as an investigator of questions in relation to consciousness studies you confine your vision to an intellectual quest however much it is based in experience from a method of practice. You state you are not a Buddhist (p. 3) and thus do not encounter the paradox that experienced Buddhists should know, viz – that they are 'not-Buddhists'. 'Buddhist' just points to a practice NOT a definition of identity. Can one practice Zen without being (called) a Zen Buddhist? By adopting this self-definition, you create a dualism of which you remain unaware. As philosopher Derrida points out, if you opt for a definition, all related definitions remain implicitly in play. This hidden opposition within self-identity continues to operate in a cryptic fashion throughout your text and ultimately causes you to hit the buffers.

ii. Up until around p. 79 the fact that you are focused so much on intellectual questions even though the method is experiential does not matter. Your investigations of mindfulness and the opening questions are exemplary. There is real dedication here and you uncovered much about what there is indeed to be discovered through this method of enquiry. I found myself in accord with virtually all your discoveries although I have followed a different orientation. I was touched by the way in which you used your retreat experiences to push forward. It was heart warming to read such close accounts of Maenllwyd, its retreat atmosphere and your personal difficulties (and I am sure readers will also be touched). You are so close to the investigation that the hidden dualism I have mentioned did not matter.

iii. On p. 79 a problematic issue begins to arise: you start 'picking and choosing', forgetting the ancient warning in the *Hsin Hsin Ming* 'The Great Way is not difficult for those who do not pick and choose'![2] It is unfortunate that you do not appear to have read Tipun's notebook[3] beyond the short excerpts used for the retreats – which were of course merely an introductory choice. There is a great deal of guidance offered in the note-book. Rather than widening your vision through a deeper acquaintance with the text, you chose to stick too tightly to your questions. Why? Presumably, it was because your prime intention was not to understand Zen in the broad but to contribute to consciousness studies through answering these questions:-an appropriate choice given your starting point, but one that imposes a limitation on what you might expect to find.

Then again, we find you rejecting a number of 'supports' offered in the tantric approach even though after a test you find them effective. In other words, your initial focus is shaping (unconsciously) your responses so that the retreat fails to flow for you. Instead, you set about testing 'hypotheses'. In other words, these choices or prejudices are a reflection of your self identification as a scientist-intellectual, the self concern and mild personal arrogance of which shuts you down on a wider openness to process. You also 'hate being kitchen assistant'. Which Sue Blackmore is this?

iv. From this point on the work becomes more complex and indeed there are difficult questions here. The exploration is admirable but there is a hidden issue emerging. You have dis-covered 'nothing' in several ways and this 'nothing' is getting a grip on you: that is you are getting attached to this 'nothing' in its several manifestations. Worse, it is shaping your answers in what can be none other than a one-sided way. Tipun remarks: 'Taking all phenomena to be like the sky one adopts a limitless attitude and goes astray with a meditation that is limitless like the sky. Taking all phenomena to be absolutely non-existent, by meditation one deviates into non-existence. Taking conscious-ness to be limitless one deviates into limitless consciousness'

(Footnote 3 p. 374). Here we have 'deviations', by which Tipun means errors on the path. You did not notice them.

v. Your intellectual insights now begin to shape your responses to the questions and the retreats and begin accumulatively to prevent further experiential insight. How far were they also shaping the quality of an ongoing awareness? Instead of using the metaphor of the string and the beads (p. 121) in the simple direct manner for which it is intended, you criticise it with an over-sophisticated argument that merely draws on one philosopher's viewpoint within Western 'Consciousness studies'. You start taking sides instead of leaving the matter open. You are reinforcing your original orientation and losing the simplicity of the Zen – 'Drop it – Let the universe do it!' approach. Your observations about threads are of course logically accurate but in the metaphor these are simply the elements of whatever is ongoing experience. Is the 'whatever-it-is' (the 'unborn', the 'original face'), out of which the multiple threads of experience (beads?) come, single or multiple? Can one tell and does it matter? The metaphor is for 'use' not for argument and attachment to a position.

Again on p. 128 you get yourself into a discriminatory argument rather than appreciating the 'use' of another metaphor.[4] You provide a detailed account of exactly what is meant by the simple words 'present moment', 'presence' and by 'awareness of awareness'. Your conclusion that such a view entails the troublesome ideas of a conscious self and things being in or out of it would be unlikely to apply to this monk highly trained in nondual Mahayana philosophy. Again – we have ideas shaping experience OR is it experience shaping ideas? Awareness of awareness means just that – awareness of awareness as it is right in the passing moment (i.e. a reflexive condition of 'now') – it does not carry the implication of anything superordinate unless one wishes it to do so.

vi. The interview on p. 132 was a disaster for both of us. I failed to show you a way beyond your intellectual fixation and you persisted in a partial viewpoint that was intellectually convincing to you. I saw it like this: you were deeply excited – 'chi' too high – and insisting on a certain explanation. This was rooted in a conviction about and attachment to 'nothing' in its several manifestations. In effect, you understood 'Form is emptiness and Emptiness is Form' but had got stuck on the left hand side of the equation without also realising that 'Emptiness is precisely Form'.

Chan Master Hongzhi (1091–1157) puts it beautifully: 'Let go of emptiness and come back to the brambly forest. Riding backwards on the ox, drunken and singing, who could dislike the misty rain pattering on your bamboo raincoat and hat?'[5]

It is as if there are two languages engaged in a game (as Wittgenstein might argue). One language identifies a self through reification of experience and speaks in words that seem to imply things. The other language apprehends the virtuality and vacuity of language and finds paradoxical words to express such puzzles. Both 'languages' express ways in which the mind responds to sensory experience (the skandhas of sensation, perception, cognition, conditioned narrative etc.). You had become fixated in the second language and it was shaping both your experience and your responses to retreat. I endeavoured to correct this one-sidedness by trying to precipitate you back into the common-sense language of self identification (Sue as a happy bog-cleaner). Since both languages are true to the way the mind operates, we were looking for a 'third' way out of the paradox. We failed and you were left in a highly argumentative if not rejecting mood. Sorry. When I said 'Technically correct' I meant that you were saying intelligible and insightful things but were far from a 'realisation going beyond'.[6]

In other words, in answer to the question 'Are you right now here in this car?' You could rightly answer either Yes or No – both are right from differing perspectives. Our minds are highly perspectival. Don't get stuck on one side or the other. What is the third place?

vii. To conclude: I will not discuss your sections on free-will or survival. I found these rather tedious. The essential part of the book preceded this and unhappily I suspect readers will lock onto these late bits and miss out the far more important preceding arguments.

Your final debunking of almost all major points in consciousness studies I enjoyed and pretty well agree with. Note that it's not that I disagree with most of your arguments, it is that from a Zen point of view all this intellection is Not It. Yet it's good fun and I am happy to see consciousness studies so consistently rubbished. I have done something similar in my forthcoming book.[7]

Finally, a bit of evolutionary psychology. Why do humans have minds like this? I think the personification and reification of the 'self' may well be due to the operation of some 'module' (which may be any functional process) that creates basic interpretations that underlie everyday languages shaping everyday experience. The identification of self as an object facilitates social interactions and also those with the 'thousand things'. It is also the basis for narratives underlying personal histories dependent on reified memories – together with all the suffering that that entails (hence the Buddha's investigations). However, all this is in ignorance of the actual processes that underlie such manifestations (psychological, chemical, physical, quanta). These can be uncovered to a degree by considering the relationship between the objective and the subjective empiricisms we have been discussing here. Why consciousness? Aha – indeed still a problem. I suspect the word needs deconstructing philosophically – but that still does not provide an answer. Leaving thought aside, we come back to life. What is Zen?

What about enlightenment? Keep going!

It is easy to pass through the eye of a needle but difficult to pass the knee of an idol.

I hope I have managed to express myself reasonably clearly. It will be good to talk in due course.

Cheers

John

[1] J.H. Crook, *The Evolution of Human Consciousness* (Oxford University Press: Oxford, 1980).

[2] Master Sheng-yen, *The Poetry of Enlightenment* (Dharma Drum Publications: New York, 1987), p. 23.

[3] J.H. Crook and J. Low, *The Yogins of Ladakh* (Motilal Banarsidass: Delhi, 1987), Chapter 17.

[4] Note Wittgenstein: – 'Ask not for the meaning. Ask for the use'.

[5] D.T. Leighton with Yi Wu, *Cultivating the Empty Field* (North Point: San Francisco, 1991), p. 46.

[6] These matters are well explored in the Lankavatara Sutra – one of the main models of mind in Zen psychology (see *The Evolution of Human Consciousness*, p. 372).

[7] J.H. Crook, *World Crisis and Buddhist Humanism* (New Age Books: Delhi, forthcoming).

Further Reading

Austin, J.H. (1998) *Zen and the Brain.* Cambridge, Mass., MIT Press

Baars, B.J. (1997) *In the Theatre of Consciousness: The Workspace of the Mind.* New York, Oxford University Press

Batchelor, S. (1998) *Buddhism without Beliefs: A Contemporary Guide to Awakening.* London, Bloomsbury

Blackmore, S. (2003) *Consciousness: An Introduction.* London, Hodder & Stoughton

Blackmore, S.J., Brelstaff, G., Nelson, K. and Troscianko, T. (1995) 'Is the Richness of Our Visual World an Illusion? Transsaccadic Memory for Complex Scenes'. *Perception,* 24, 1075–81

Chalmers, D.J. (1995) 'Facing Up to the Problem of Consciousness'. *Journal of Consciousness Studies,* 2, 200–19

Churchland, P. (2007) *Neurophilosophy at Work.* Cambridge, Cambridge University Press

Crick, F. (1994) *The Astonishing Hypothesis.* New York, Scribner's

Crook, J.H. (1980) *The Evolution of Human Consciousness.* Oxford, Oxford University Press

Crook, J.H. (1991) *Catching a Feather on a Fan: Zen Retreat with Master Sheng Yen.* Shaftesbury, Dorset, Element Books

Crook, J.H. and Low, J. (1987) *The Yogins of Ladakh: A Pilgrimage among the Hermits of the Buddhist Himalayas.* Delhi, Motilal Banarsidass

Damasio, A. (1999) *The Feeling of What Happens: Body, Emotion and the Making of Consciousness.* London, Heinemann

Dennett, D.C. (1985) *Elbow Room: The Varieties of Free Will Worth Wanting.*
     Oxford, Oxford University Press

Dennett, D.C. (1991) *Consciousness Explained.* London, Little, Brown &
     Co.

James, W. (1890) *The Principles of Psychology,* London, Macmillan

Libet, B. (1985) 'Unconscious Cerebral Initiative and the Role of
     Conscious Will in Voluntary Action', *Behavioral and Brain Sciences,* 8,
     529–39. See also the many commentaries in the same issue, 539–66,
     and *BBS,* 10, 318–21

Metzinger, T. (ed.) (2000) *Neural Correlates of Consciousness,* Cambridge,
     Mass., MIT Press

Milner, A.D. and Goodale, M.A. (1995) *The Visual Brain in Action,*
     Oxford, Oxford University Press

Nagel, T. (1974) 'What Is It Like to Be a Bat?', *Philosophical Review,* 83,
     435–50

Noë, A. (2002) *Is the Visual World a Grand Illusion?* Thorverton, UK,
     Imprint Academic

O'Regan, J.K. and Noë, A. (2001) 'A Sensorimotor Account of Vision
     and Visual Consciousness', *Behavioral and Brain Sciences,* 24(5),
     939–1011

Parfit, D. (1984) *Reasons and Persons,* Oxford, Clarendon Press

Rahula, W. (1974) *What the Buddha Taught* (revised edition). New York,
     Grove Press/Atlantic Books

Varela, F.J. and Shear, J. (1999) *The View from Within: First Person
     Approaches to the Study of Consciousness.* Thorverton, Devon, Imprint
     Academic

Velmans, M. (2000) *Understanding Consciousness.* London, Routledge

Wegner, D. (2002) *The Illusion of Conscious Will,* Cambridge, Mass., MIT
     Press

Index

42

Deep Thought on Life, the Universe, and Everything

Deftly interweaving the thoughts of the greatest minds of all time, from Socrates to Monty Python, Mark Vernon provides a platter of witty yet profound discussions on work, love, eternal life, sex, and happiness. From the allure of cats to the nature of wisdom, this rip-roaring read is the perfect companion for the armchair philosopher, and proves that even a little introspection can transform our lives for the better!

978-1-85168-560-8 - PB
£9.99/ $14.95

"A joy to read, yielding both wisdom and delight in perfectly sized portions. A trip to the supermarket will never be the same again."
Professor Richard Schoch – Queen Mary, University of London and author of *The Secrets of Happiness*

"How refreshing... an antidote to those happiness gurus who peddle off-the-shelf recipes for the good life." **Claire Fox** – Director of the Institute of Ideas, and panellist on BBC Radio 4's *The Moral Maze*

MARK VERNON is a writer, broadcaster, and journalist. He is the author of numerous books including *Science, Religion and the Meaning of Life* and *The Philosophy of Friendship*. He has a PhD in philosophy, as well as degrees in theology and physics, and is an Honorary Research Fellow at Birkbeck College, University of London.

Browse all our titles at
www.oneworld-publications.com O N E W O R L D

A Beginner's Guide to The Brain

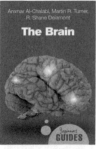

Ammar Al-Chalabi, Martin R. Turner, R. Shane Delamont

The Brain

Beginners
GUIDES

978-1-85168-594-3
£9.99/ $14.95

Using the very latest research in neuroscience this lively introduction explains how 1.4kg of wet grey tissue can not only control all of our bodily functions, thoughts, and behaviours, but also house the very essence of who we are.

"A virtuoso performance! The book is technical, easy to read and entertaining." **Garth Nicholson** – Associate Professor of Medical Genetics, University of Sydney

"A concise primer that summarizes the fascinating complexity of the brain in a memorable and refreshingly graspable manner." **Robert Brown** – Professor of Neurology, Harvard Medical School

AMMAR AL-CHALABI is an Honorary Consultant Neurologist at King's College Hospital and Senior Lecturer at King's College London.

MARTIN R. TURNER is a Specialist Registrar in Neurology at the John Radcliffe Hospital in Oxford, and a Clinical Tutorial Fellow at Green College, Oxford University.

R. SHANE DELAMONT is a Consultant Neurologist at King's College Hospital.

Browse further titles at
www.oneworld-publications.com

Beginners
GUIDES

A Beginner's Guide to The Buddha

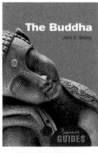

978-1-85168-601-8
£9.99/ $14.95

In this authoritative biography, John Strong presents the Buddha's story the way Buddhists have told it – from accounts of his previous lives, and the story of his birth and upbringing, through to his enlightenment, deathbed deeds, and ongoing presence in the relics that he left behind.

"Among the many biographies of the Buddha available to the general reader, John Strong's remains the best. It draws from a vast body of sources with sensitivity and insight to paint a fascinating portrait of a towering figure." **Donald S. Lopez** – Arthur E. Link Distinguished University Professor of Buddhist and Tibetan Studies, University of Michigan

"Strong's book is clearly the best available 'Guide for Beginners'." **Frank Reynolds** – Professor Emeritus of History of Religions and Buddhist Studies, University of Chicago

JOHN S. STRONG is Charles A. Dana Professor of Religious Studies at Bates College in Maine, USA. He is the author of four other books on Buddhism.

Browse further titles at
www.oneworld-publications.com